Island
Bound

Deb
Loughead

Published by Pearson Education Limited, Edinburgh Gate, Harlow, Essex, CM20 2JE.

www.pearsonschools.co.uk

First published by Pearson New Zealand
a division of Pearson New Zealand Ltd
67 Apollo Drive, Rosedale, North Shore 0632, New Zealand
Associated companies throughout the world

Text © Pearson Education New Zealand 2007
Original edition edited by Lucy Armour
Original edition designed by Jane Cameron and Ruby-Anne Fenning
This edition designed by Sara Rafferty

The right of Deb Loughead to be identified as author of this work has been
asserted by her in accordance with the Copyright, Designs and Patents Act 1988.

First published 2007
This edition published 2013

17 16 15
10 9 8 7 6 5 4 3 2

British Library Cataloguing in Publication Data
A catalogue record for this book is available from the British Library

ISBN 978 0 435 14424 1

Printed in Malaysia (CTP-VVP)

Acknowledgements
We would like to thank Bangor Central Integrated Primary School, Northern Ireland; Bishop
Henderson Church of England Primary School, Somerset; Bletchingdon Parochial Church
of England Primary School, Oxfordshire; Brookside Community Primary School, Somerset;
Bude Park Primary School, Hull; Cheddington Combined School, Buckinghamshire; Dair
House Independent School, Buckinghamshire; Glebe Infant School, Gloucestershire;
Henley Green Primary School, Coventry; Lovelace Primary School, Surrey; Our Lady of
Peace Junior School, Slough; Tackley Church of England Primary School, Oxfordshire;
and Twyford Church of England School, Buckinghamshire for their invaluable help in the
development and trialling of the Bug Club resources.

Every effort has been made to contact copyright holders of material reproduced in this book.
Any omissions will be rectified in subsequent printings if notice is given to the publishers.

A division of Pearson New Zealand Ltd

Contents

Chapter One

"Hannah? Are you studying? Can I come in?"

Hannah Hawthorne had been trying her best to ignore the gentle rapping on her bedroom door. She was pretty sure she knew who it was, and exactly what he wanted.

"Come on in, Dad," she said finally, trying to disguise the reluctance in her voice.

When Hannah's dad crossed the room and handed her the stack of colourful brochures, he had a huge smile stretched across his face.

"What's this?" she asked him, doing her best to sound as if she cared.

"Take a look, honey," he said, his smile growing even broader until it seemed to swallow his whole face. At that particular moment, Hannah didn't feel like smiling. She had a sinking feeling, somewhere deep in the pit of her stomach.

"I'm kind of busy right now, Dad." She fanned out the brochures in her hand, flipping through them distractedly, then laying them down on her desk. "I'll look at them later, maybe when I've finished my homework."

Dad's face sagged with a disappointment he couldn't conceal, but Hannah hardened her heart. She knew *exactly* what he was excited about and it was having the opposite effect on her. Her insides were churning as if she were on a Ferris wheel.

As her dad slipped quietly out of the room, pulling the door shut behind him with a soft click, Hannah closed the book she was reading and slid the brochures over. The one on the top showed a picture of a rocky cove, sparkling turquoise water, an aqua sky and people in bathing suits frolicking in the sand. She shivered, but she wasn't sure if it was with dread or delight.

Someone rapped on her bedroom door again, but this time it was more urgent. Hannah slapped her book down over the top of the brochure.

"Who's there?" she called.

"It's Mum. Can I come in?"

The door creaked open before Hannah could reply and she quickly opened her novel again, burying her face in it, trying to look preoccupied. Her mother padded over and sat down on the edge of her bed. Hannah couldn't look at her, dreading what she was about to hear. She squeezed her eyes shut and listened.

"Your father's very disappointed," said her mother. "He was really counting on a positive reaction from you. He knows how much you love the island."

"To *visit*," blurted Hannah. "*Not* to live there. *Never* to *live* there."

"Your brother's ecstatic. He can't wait to leave."

"Jake's only twelve. He won't have so much trouble making new friends."

"Neither will you, Hannah." Her mother tried to squeeze Hannah's shoulder, but Hannah pushed her hand away. "It's not forever, honey. Just for two years. That's not very long."

"It's a long time when you're *my* age. By the time I get back, all my friends will have forgotten about me."

"That's not true." Her mother's voice was losing its soft, patient tone. Now there was something hard there. Something hard and blunt. "I think you're just looking for excuses. You know how much your dad was counting on your cooperation. Please don't do this to him."

"What? I'm not *doing* anything. Why are you getting mad at *me*?"

Hannah's mother sighed and shook her soft brown curls. A little furrow had formed on her forehead and her dark eyes glinted with impatience.

"Think about this long and hard, Hannah. Think about what a wonderful experience it could be. Think about how much you'll learn and the people you'll meet. Think about how happy you'll make your father if you just walk out of this room with a smile on your face and say that you don't mind going. He feels bad enough already and your attitude is making him feel worse."

"I'll think about it," mumbled Hannah. With another impatient sigh, her mother strode from the room, yanking the door shut behind her.

As she flipped through the pile of booklets and brochures, Hannah let her mind wander back to Bermuda. Each picture triggered a new memory. She had been travelling there for thirteen years, every summer since she was born. She knew how the sand felt, powdery pink and warm under her feet. She knew what it was like to swim in the turquoise sea, and to sit in the shade of a pawpaw tree for hours, reading or watching sailboats bobbing out in the harbour.

She knew all about the pastel shades of the limestone-roofed houses that edged the shores. She'd been lulled to sleep by the trill of tree frogs and awakened by the shrill cry of the yellow kiskadee bird. Hannah knew about pink buses and motor scooters that buzzed like busy bees along the winding roads of the island. After all, she had spent a month each summer immersed in the culture of her mother's native land. But she wasn't sure that she wanted to *live* there.

Hannah sat at her desk and thought about it until dinner time that evening. She thought about it until she couldn't think any more. At last, she got out a pen and paper and made a list with two columns.

Bermuda: Good Points
* Plenty of sunshine
* Beautiful beaches
* Dolphins (I love them!)

* *Tropical fish (wow!)*
* *Amazing birds!*
* *Palm trees and fragrant flowers everywhere*
* *Possibly new friends??????*
* *Only two years*

Bermuda: Bad Points

* *Too much sunshine*
* *Sand in your shoes*
* *Lizards and giant toads (ew, ew, ew!)*
* *Massive poisonous jellyfish (yikes)*
* *No robins or blue jays!*
* *No maple trees and no snow! (I love snow!)*
* *Possibly no friends!!!!!!*
* *Two whole years!!!!!!*

Usually by making a list she could make a decision, but this time it hadn't helped at all. By the time she heard her mother calling her down to dinner, she was more confused than ever. She plodded down the stairs and plopped down in her regular seat at the kitchen table. Thin December twilight seeped weakly through the windows and outside the bare trees seemed to shiver in the frosty chill. *One more thing to add to the list*, thought Hannah.

Leaves on trees all year round! But no snow. Never ever any snow at all. And that stinks.

Hannah kept her eyes glued on her plate all through dinner. She ate her tuna casserole slowly, noodle by noodle, and lost her appetite before she was half-finished. No one was speaking. Everyone was tangled up in silent thoughts. Even Jake, who never seemed to stop talking, had his lips zipped for a change.

Hannah knew why. Everyone wanted to go except for her. If she could only look up and smile. If she could only say that she was happy about her father's job transfer, that she didn't mind moving to Bermuda, that it was only for two years after all, then all of their faces would light up like Christmas trees. They'd all start chattering and everything would be fine again.

Hannah swallowed another forkful of tuna casserole and struggled to get it down, almost as if a strong hand were gripping her throat. Then she took a deep breath and looked around at her family, one by one. "So? When do we leave, anyway?"

Sure enough, Jake's face lit up like a Christmas tree. And now her parents were beaming, too.

Hannah tried to smile back at them, but for some reason she felt as if she were sucking on a wedge of lemon. And she didn't like the taste at all.

Chapter Two

Hannah usually liked the plane ride. She liked the way the huge jet sped up on the runway so that Toronto International Airport and its busy ground crew, zipping around in their little luggage carts, refuelling planes and loading cargo, all became one colourful blur. She liked the way they slanted upward, airborne at last, and everything beneath them shrank to toy size as they rose above the clouds and headed south. *For Bermuda.*

They would circle over Lake Ontario and Dad would point out the CN Tower and Skydome, and busy highways and byways. They would fly over Hamilton, Ontario, and he would point out the Burlington Skyway and soon Niagara Falls. Then there'd be mountains and rivers, farmland that looked like patchwork quilts and many more miniature towns and cities.

Hannah usually liked to think about the people below them, going about their business, making breakfast, driving around in cars, going shopping or to the library, sitting in dentist chairs, mouths wide open, fishing in streams, playing the piano, weeding the garden, hunched in front of computers in tall office towers that looked like so many bee boxes, while she lounged back in her airline seat and waited to land in the most beautiful place in the world. *To visit on summer vacation. Not to live for two whole years.*

This time Hannah didn't even glance out of the window at the snowy city below them. She kept her seatbelt buckled and fastened her eyes on the seat in front of her.

"Fair weather ahead," the first officer told them. "Say goodbye to the Toronto winter. We're headed for a balmy 23 degrees Celsius. Nothing beats a Bermuda December!"

"Did you hear that?" Jake was bouncing in his seat. "Did you pack my bathing suit, Mum? Can I swim?"

"I doubt it," she said. "The ocean will be a little too cool. You've never been here at this time of year. From what I remember as a kid, the ocean gets chilly during the winter months. And besides, we're just going down for a few days, to look for somewhere to live. We might not even make it to the beach."

"Can't we stay with Belterre and Willie for Christmas? Do we *have* to come back? Do we, Mum? Do we?" Jake tugged persistently on the sleeve of Mum's jacket.

"Yes." The word snapped off Hannah's tongue. It was the first one out of her mouth since she'd buckled her seatbelt half an hour earlier. "We have to be home in time for Christmas. Nana's expecting us for dinner on Christmas Day. And anyway, Christmas would stink without snow and cold weather."

Hannah's mother's voice was patient. "Well it can be quite beautiful, actually, with the hibiscus hedges and their colourful trumpets and vines of purple bougainvillea in bloom. And the poinsettias – the Christmas flower. Great big bushes of them in red and white, growing alongside the road instead of in a pot on the dining room table like we have at home. It's amazing!"

"Belterre will want us to stay, won't she?"

"Of course she will, Jake. But we can't. Only

until the 23rd. That gives us almost six whole days." Dad reached across the seats and pinched Jake's thigh in a gentle horse bite. "My mum would be pretty disappointed if we weren't sitting around the table on Christmas day in Toronto. And so would all your cousins, don't you think?"

"Guess so," agreed Jake, reluctantly.

Hannah sat back in the comfortable seat and closed her eyes. Only six days. That couldn't be nearly enough time to find somewhere to live. And if they couldn't find a place to live down there, maybe they wouldn't have to move to Bermuda after all. Maybe Dad could move down there alone for two years and come back on the weekend every once in a while, and on holidays, like Easter and Christmas.

Maybe he could live in one of the island hotels. Maybe his company would pay. Maybe Hannah and Jake and Mum could go down and visit Dad once in a while, just so he wouldn't be so lonely. And maybe they could even spend the whole summer with him. Maybe *that* would make him happy. *Maybe. Maybe. Maybe.*

Hannah dozed off full of *maybes* and woke up with Jake's pointy elbow nudging her in the ribs.

"They're serving breakfast, Hannah. The flight attendant wants to know if you'd like sausage and eggs or pancakes."

"Nothing. I'm not hungry."

"You sure, sweetie?" asked the flight attendant, smiling down at her. "There's a meal here for you if you'd like it. And I have orange and grapefruit juice. Would you just like some cereal instead? Or some fruit?"

Hannah sighed heavily, and then noticed that everyone was staring at her. Dad was frowning and Mum had something that looked like concern knitted into the lines on her forehead.

"Okay. I'll have the pancakes. And orange juice. And a cup of tea, too."

Everyone smiled. Hannah sat back in her seat, rolling her eyes as the attendant set the tray on her table. She put on her headphones and tuned into a rock station so she would have an excuse to ignore everyone, and then began to chew slowly on the soggy pancakes, floating in a sea of too much syrup.

Hannah was always surprised at how short the flight was. Soon they were circling the narrow, fish-hook-shaped island and she was looking down on turquoise water and pale beaches. Sailboats out in the harbour and beyond sliced across the surface of a smooth ocean barely ruffled by waves.

The flight attendants collected headphones and newspapers, stray glasses and cups. The seatbelt light flashed. Hannah hadn't touched hers since she'd buckled it nearly three hours earlier.

Jake was wriggling in his seat. "I can see the roads. I can see buses and taxis and motor scooters. There's a fort. And a golf course."

"My favourite one," said Dad, grinning.

The plane touched down with a familiar bump and rolled to a stop. They gathered their flight bags from the overhead compartment and Hannah slung her precious backpack over her shoulders. It was stuffed with reminders of home, things that she liked to take with her everywhere, comfort when she wasn't sleeping in her own room. She offered the flight attendants a feeble smile as she stepped through the door, and then blinked in the sudden flood of light. Warm Bermuda sunshine caressed her freckled face and sandy blonde hair.

"We're here," she whispered as she started down the steps.

Chapter Three

They cleared customs within half an hour and were soon standing in front of the airport, watching for a taxi and gazing across the sparkling waters of Castle Harbour.

"Here's Willie now," said Dad, taking a piece of luggage in each hand. "Everyone grab something so he won't have to get out of the cab to help us."

"Hey ho, everybody! Right on time as usual!" Willie stuck his face out of the window, grinning wide and bright. His mass of tight, springy curls, as soft as a lamb's coat, seemed a little more silvery than it had been in the summer and his dark face was deeply etched with smile lines.

"How was the flight, folks?"

"Flawless," said Mum, as she helped Dad pack the back of the van with their luggage.

"And how're those two godkids of mine?" Willie put his hand out the window to ruffle Jake's head.

"Awesome!" Jake slid the door open, climbed into the back and wrapped his arms around Willie's broad shoulders from behind. "I couldn't wait to get here. Don't you think it would be great if we could stay for Christmas?"

"Now that would be something, wouldn't it? Belterre would sure like that!"

"Jake." Mum's voice sounded a warning. "You know we can't."

"I can stay alone. I won't mind …"

"Jake," said Dad, as he slammed the van door and settled in beside Willie. "Lay off."

"Hey, the boy loves the island. Nothing wrong with that." Willie steered his taxi out on to the causeway and soon they were surrounded by stretches of shallow water in vivid shades of azure and aquamarine.

"This is the place where tourists really start to gasp when they're visiting the island for the first time," Willie told them, as he always did. "Never seen water such a colour before, they always say. Can't wait to get their toes in it!"

"Neither can I!" Jake said. "How's the water, Willie? Can I swim?"

"It's not too bad. And the air's warm. You're a tough kid. You won't mind it."

Mum leaned forward in her seat and touched Willie's shoulder. "How's Belterre?" she asked him. "Feisty as ever?"

"Course. That woman won't ever change. She's cooked up a big pot of conch chowder for supper. Knows how much the kids love it. And you loved it as a kid, too, didn't you, Celia?"

"I still love it," said Mum. "My favourite island meal. Can't wait."

"It's spiny lobster season, too, isn't it? Any of that around, Willie?" Dad was rubbing his stomach as though he were half-starved.

"Oh, I'm sure we can find some, Dave." Willie's chuckle was loud and hearty. "Same old appetite, huh? Some things never change."

"It's the island air. I keep telling you, Willie."

"I think it's Belterre's cooking, Dad," said Jake. "You always pig out when we're in Bermuda."

Everyone laughed, even Hannah. They drove past the familiar landmarks along the narrow, winding roads – the sprawling pastel-coloured homes, each with its own peculiar name, like Seaview, Petrel Perch or Whistling Frog; the restaurants, beaches and hotels. Hannah sat back in her seat and tried to relax.

She opened a window and let the warm island air blow on to her face and ruffle her hair. The flower-bright hedges and lush tropical shrubbery flashed by in a blur and soon she closed her eyes and listened to the buzz of motor scooters, the toot of horns and the low murmur of conversation. Up front, her parents were talking about moving to Bermuda and Willie was saying how excited Belterre was that Celia would be on the island again. How it would be just like old times when she was a little girl.

Hannah's mother, Celia, had grown up in Bermuda and moved to Canada when she was just a little older than Hannah was now. She'd attended high school and then university in Toronto, but some of her fondest memories were of growing up in Bermuda, of sunshine and sand and warm ocean water.

Celia liked to tell Hannah and Jake tales of life by the sea, about sailing out in the harbour and swimming with all sorts of strange and wonderful fish in a brilliant kaleidoscope of colours. She reeled off their exotic names – angelfish, parrot and squirrel fish, blue tang. She described the wild typhoons that came roaring up from the south and soaked the island so thoroughly that the streets became rivers and the palms swayed in the wind as if made of rubber. She enthralled them with yarns of pirates and shipwrecks so many times that they almost knew them by heart. And when she finished one Bermuda tale, they would always beg for another.

Celia's mother had died when she was a little girl and her father had raised her alone, with the help of Belterre, who was her nanny. Belterre had been the one who cooked for Celia and her father. She had taken Celia to school on her first day, comforted her when she cried, taken care of their cool, bright house by the sea and filled it up with laughter and joy. When Celia and her father moved to Canada, Belterre had hugged Celia tightly and cried for hours.

Now, whenever they visited Bermuda, Hannah's family stayed with Belterre and her husband Willie in their small home in

Southampton Parish, for weeks at a time during the summer months.

Belterre, whose name meant "beautiful land", treated Hannah and Jake like her own grand-children. She told them stories, sang them songs, baked cookies and kept plenty of goodies at hand. And she still sobbed whenever they had to fly back to Canada, hugging them against her plump bosom and telling them how much she wished they could stay and didn't always have to fly home after a few weeks.

"And it looks like her wish will be coming true pretty soon," Hannah said to herself.

Jake heard her. "Who are you talking to?" he asked. "Yourself?"

"Well not to you, that's for sure," snapped Hannah. "You always yap so much, no one else ever gets a chance to talk."

"What's with you? Did a bee fly up your nose? You've been a crab ever since we got on the plane. Don't you like it here?" Jake stared at her with an expression of outraged disbelief. "How can you not like it here?"

"I never said I don't like it," hissed Hannah, keeping her voice low so that Willie wouldn't hear them above her parents' voices. "But we really don't know many people here, do we? We spend all our time with Belterre's family and we never get to know any other kids. And now, right after Christmas, we have to rent out our house in Toronto and move everything over here for *two years*. Doesn't that bother you at all? To just abandon all our friends and everything else and move all the way down here to live? You can't tell me that it doesn't bother you!"

Jake cocked his head and frowned. "I guess I didn't really think about it that much. Dad said we were coming, and it sounded cool, and I know we're going back some day. So I guess I'm just going with the flow, like my teacher always says."

"But what about your friends? Aren't you going to miss them?"

"Sure. But I'll make new ones here. It's not hard to make friends."

"Well, maybe for you it isn't."

"What about Maya? You get along with her."

Hannah grinned when she thought about Belterre's bubbly granddaughter. "She's sixteen though. She's got her own friends. She won't want me tagging along with her."

Jake shook his head at her. "You worry way too much."

"And I suppose boys never worry about anything at all, huh?" said Hannah.

Jake shrugged. "It's not that we don't think about stuff. Usually we just don't let stuff bother us as much as girls do. You should try it some time!"

Hannah wrinkled up her nose in disgust and turned to face the window and the swift blur of azure sea and verdant palms.

Before long they had reached Southampton Parish and were turning from the Tribe Road into the narrow driveway of Belterre and Willie's house. Stones crunched under the tyres as Willie steered his cab into the front yard. The whitewashed stone house gleamed in the sunshine, all its navy blue shutters pushed open to welcome the breeze. A huge poinsettia bush was blooming with flames of Christmas red.

"See!" said Mum. "Didn't I tell you about the poinsettias? Isn't that beautiful! It's never in bloom when we visit for summer vacation!"

Suddenly, the heavy cedar door burst open and Belterre was flying along the pathway, apron flapping, flowered dress in full sail before the breeze, a dazzling smile lighting up her face.

"You're here!" she cried, wrapping the children in her pillowy embrace. "And pretty soon you'll all be here to stay! I can hardly wait for that day!"

Hannah worked on her best smile, but it felt as if she were sucking on that lemon again. She tried to force her trembling lips to curl upwards when they only wanted to twist down into an unhappy frown.

Chapter Four

Belterre and Willie didn't stop chattering right through lunch. As Hannah and her family sat gathered around the kitchen table, slurping conch chowder and munching on home-made biscuits, they listened to their merry voices reciting how delighted they were to have them back.

"It's the perfect Christmas gift," Belterre told them, as she whisked about the kitchen making sure they had enough to eat. Every few minutes, she wrapped her strong arms around Hannah's mother and hugged her hard. "I still can't believe you're actually here in December. And that you're soon coming home to stay. You don't know how happy this is making me!"

It's not making me happy. This isn't home and it never will be. The thought invaded Hannah's head like ants at a picnic. *Toronto is home and it always will be, and that's where I want to stay. I will never be happy here, no matter how hard I try.* The words scurried around in her head and she couldn't stamp them out. She stared miserably into her bowl of chowder, hoping that no one would notice.

"Oh, I think we know how happy you are, Bel," Willie said. "You'd better stop squeezing Celia so much. She won't be able to swallow her soup."

"It's okay, Willie. I miss Belterre's hugs. I look forward to them all year and, when I get here, I just can't get enough of them. They're a kind of therapy."

"You see, Willie!" Belterre slapped her thigh and laughed out loud. "I told you my hugs could do a body good."

Hannah tried to smile, as she usually did whenever Belterre laughed. The sound of her laughter was infectious. There was something musical about it that reminded Hannah of wind chimes, something warm and welcoming. But her flimsy smile withered away after a second and Belterre knew instantly that something was wrong. She pulled up a chair beside Hannah, plopped her wide bottom down on it, and took Hannah's chin in her hand.

"What's wrong, child? Usually you never stop smiling from the moment you walk through that door. I've seen you smiling in your sleep when you're here. Tell Belterre what's wrong."

"Nothing's wrong, Bel," said Hannah, offering her best effort at a smile. "See. I'm smiling."

"If that's a smile, then I'm a giant toad! Now something's wrong and I know it. I raised your mother and you're just like her. I know when something's bothering you. Are you going to tell me or are you just going to keep on pretending that you're happy?"

"I'll tell you what's wrong with her. She doesn't want to be here." The words burst out of Jake's mouth before Hannah could answer Belterre. "She doesn't want to live here at all. She wants to stay in Toronto with her friends. Right, Hannah?"

Everyone was staring at her. She felt a slow flush creep up her neck and begin to burn her cheeks.

"That's not true, Jake," Hannah murmured into her bowl. The last thing she wanted to do was hurt the feelings of these two wonderful people who meant so much to her family.

Belterre's dark, attentive eyes had grown wide at Jake's revelation and now she was frowning. "It's not true at all, Belterre," mumbled Hannah, unconvincingly.

"Yes it is," said Jake, between bites of biscuit. "You told me on the way here in Willie's cab."

Hannah glanced up at him, her face burning brighter. He was grinning and there were bits of food stuck in his teeth. She wanted to slap him. She kicked him under the table instead.

"Ouch!" he yelped. "Why didja do that, Hannah?"

"What's going on here?" Their father slapped both hands flat on the table with a loud whack to attract their attention, as he always did when he tried to stop an argument. It worked. "Would someone like to explain to me what the problem is?"

"I think I know." Belterre's voice was gentle. "And I think this is upsetting Hannah enough. We don't need to keep shooting questions at her. She'll answer us when she's ready. Right, honey?"

"Right," whispered Hannah. "I think I'll go sit out in the garden for a while." She knew that the eyes of everyone in the room were locked on her as she slipped out through the back door without another word.

At the back of the house, facing the sea, Belterre's flower gardens blazed with vivid blossoms that cascaded over low walls and filled the air with a soothing perfume. Bougainvillea vines spilled through the fence at the edge of the garden and crept up the limestone walls of the house. The pawpaw tree stretched its slender green fingers, creating a wide patch of shade in a corner.

This was where Hannah always liked to sit and watch the ocean, on a creaky old cedar bench that Willie had built many years ago. It was grey and weathered now, a perfect thinking spot when you had something on your mind. It had been there for as long as Hannah could remember, reaching out its welcoming arms, offering her comfort and solitude.

The breeze licked the surface of the turquoise ocean, ruffling it with small whitecaps. There weren't any sailboats out there today; gales could blow in suddenly at this time of year and sailors were cautious. But seabirds tipped and twirled, dipped and dived, and somewhere nearby a kiskadee was calling. Hannah wondered how she could be so forlorn in such a beautiful place.

I've got to change my attitude, she told herself. *It's making everyone uncomfortable. I've got to keep reminding myself that it's only for two years. Only for two years. Only for two years.* She repeated it, hoping she would believe it, as the wind brushed her face and whispered ocean music in her ears.

The buzz of an approaching motor scooter cut into her thoughts and she sat up straight and listened. People didn't venture along this road very often, unless they were lost. It didn't lead anywhere – only to the few quaint cottages that squatted along the edge of the ocean. Hannah knew at once who it must be. Maya.

She hurried to the garden gate and leaned over, watching for Belterre's granddaughter. It was a tradition. Hannah always waited for Maya at the gate, opening it for her so she could steer the scooter inside. Once she had ridden a bicycle, but now Maya had her own scooter, bought with her own money earned from summer jobs working at a hotel.

Maya turned into the driveway, cut the engine and wheeled her scooter through the gate.

"Hannah Banana!" she shrieked and Hannah couldn't help but grin.

"Maya Papaya!" Hannah shrieked back.

Maya leaned the bike against the wall and wrapped her long, slim arms around Hannah in a welcoming embrace. "So glad you're here," she whispered near Hannah's ear.

"You changed your hair!" said Hannah, admiring the neat rows of short, tight knots that criss-crossed Maya's scalp.

"Yeah. I didn't like it long any more. This is so much easier to take care of. Hey! Can I put your hair in all those teeny braids again? It looks so good like that. How are you, anyway? I can't believe you're here in December. Please say that you're staying for Christmas."

"No. We have to go home. And yes, you can definitely put my hair in braids again. Nobody else can do it like you can!"

Maya hooked her arm through Hannah's and dragged her over to the old cedar bench. It was wide enough for both of them and they squeezed together to chat, just as they always did.

"Is it true?" Maya grasped both of Hannah's hands and gazed earnestly into her eyes. "Are you really going to move here?"

Hannah caught her lower lip between her teeth and nodded.

"That's amazing! You must be so excited." Then she frowned and pushed her face closer to Hannah's. "Why aren't you smiling, Hannah? It almost looks as if you don't want to live here. But I know you love the island."

Maya was so perceptive. She could read a person's face, know their innermost thoughts, without even hearing them. Hannah had always admired that quality in her – the way she could pierce her secret thoughts, just like Belterre. For a moment, Hannah couldn't answer.

"Tell me," said Maya. "Because you know you're going to sooner or later. You always do."

"Okay, I'm not thrilled with the idea," admitted Hannah. "But would you be, if you had to leave this place? Somewhere that you're so used to. Your home and your friends. How would you like it?"

"I'd love it!"

Hannah was startled by her reply.

"In fact, I plan on travelling around the world, first chance I get. Working on a cruise ship or as a flight attendant. It would be amazing!"

Hannah laced her fingers together in a tight knot on her lap. No one, it seemed, could understand exactly how she felt. Perhaps no one ever would.

Chapter Five

That night after supper, when the reminiscing about good times was over and Maya had ridden her scooter home, Hannah lay tucked up in the tiny room that had once belonged to Belterre's daughter, Maya's mother. The house was quiet now and through the open window Hannah could hear the soft sigh of the ocean and the whispering breeze in the palm trees.

Hannah usually felt good in the cosy bed, knowing she was in her favourite place and anticipating the adventures she would share with Maya during her visit, the trips to the beach, the ferry boat rides into Hamilton. But this visit, she knew, would be spent house-hunting with her parents and a feeling of dread gathered in the pit of her stomach. When they found a house, the For Rent sign would go up on their property at home in Toronto and she would have to face the fact that there was no turning back. How would she ever fit into this new country? How would she ever adjust to all the new people and to leaving her friends behind?

When she finally fell asleep, her cheeks were damp with tears, tears of misery and guilt for feeling so unhappy and letting everyone down.

The next morning, Hannah's eyes flew open to the shriek of a kiskadee. It was perched on her window sill, boldly peering in at her like a feathered bandit in its black mask. It shrieked again, startling her all over again.

"What do you want, you cheeky thing?" she asked, rubbing her eyes and sitting up in bed. The bird cocked its head and stared at her with its dark, clever eyes, almost as though it might answer. "I don't have any food. You should fly over to one of the hotels. A tourist is sure to feed you some crumbs over there."

By the time Hannah had washed, dressed and shuffled sleepily into the kitchen, the small house was bustling with activity. Willie was scrambling eggs, Belterre was stirring something in a bowl and Mum and Dad were sipping coffee as they pored over the estate agents' pages. Jake was at the table, stuffing himself with fresh scones and loquat jam, and Maya sat opposite him, a wide grin plastered across her face. There was a girl sitting beside her, a girl Hannah had never seen before.

"Good morning, sunshine!" Maya greeted her.

"Did you sleep well?" asked Belterre.

"Right up until the kiskadee yelled in my ear," murmured Hannah. She sat down at the table and stared at its surface, reluctant to face everyone again. After the scene in the kitchen at lunch yesterday, they had stolen glances at her all evening, tiptoeing around her feelings, careful not to upset her. Even Jake had backed off and that was unusual for him.

"That bold little fellow hangs around here all the time. Ever since I fed him a few bread crusts one day. Now he thinks he's a member of the family." Belterre's mellow laughter filled the room and Hannah dared to look up. They were all looking at her again, of course, hoping that Belterre's lighthearted touch might help her to feel better. Hannah was sorry that she'd ever mentioned her feelings to anyone. Somehow it was easier to hide the way she felt, to pretend, rather have everyone treat her as though she had a sign on her forehead that read Handle with Care.

"This is my friend Cassie," said Maya. "You guys are about the same age. I thought you might like to say hi."

"Hi!" said Cassie in a sprightly voice. She was a small girl with bright blue eyes and long hair as black and shiny as a crow's feathers, tied back in a neat ponytail.

"We're going to the beach later," said Maya. "Would you like to come, Hannah?"

Everyone stared at her, waiting for her to answer, hoping, probably, that an outing to the beach would cheer her up.

"I guess so," she said. When she looked over at her parents, they both had strained smiles on their faces. Belterre was frowning, the way she always did whenever anyone mentioned a trip to the beach.

"Just stay out of the water," snapped Belterre, glancing away when everyone turned to look at her. "It's mighty cold this time of year. I'm sure I don't have to remind you. Not good for swimming at all."

Hannah stepped out of the little cottage and stood blinking in the bright warm sunshine.

"Where's your motor scooter, Maya?"

"I rode my trusty old bike over," she said. "And so did Cassie. My granny said you could borrow her bike so that we could all ride to the beach. How does that sound?"

"Just fine, I guess," said Hannah. She threw her backpack over her shoulders. "I didn't know Belterre had a bike. Where does she keep it?"

"Right in here." Maya was opening the door of a rickety shed tucked away beside the house. When she wheeled it out, Hannah heard Cassie stifle a giggle behind her hand. Her eyes opened wide as she stared at the ancient bicycle with its dusty, rusted frame and huge wicker basket on the back. The tyres were flat and it looked as if it hadn't been ridden in twenty years.

"You don't expect me to ride that thing, do you, Maya?"

"What's wrong with it?" Maya was grinning,

too. "It just needs some air in the tyres and I brought a pump. We don't have far to go."

"She'll look like that old lady in *The Wizard of Oz*," said Cassie, giggling again. "Pedalling away with Toto in her basket on the back."

Hannah's eyes narrowed. She recalled Maya's words when she'd introduced her to Cassie. *I thought you might like to say hi.* So far there wasn't much she liked about Cassie. As far as she was concerned, Maya could keep her island friends to herself.

"I'm not riding on that thing. I'll fall off and kill myself. Anyway, I don't know my way around the island, with all the crazy twists and turns and everybody driving the wrong way. At least you two are used to the roads and traffic. I'd be too nervous riding on a shaky old thing like that. Besides … it's just so ugly."

Maya and Cassie were doubled over laughing. Laughing at her and the stupid bike they expected her to ride. Hannah tightened her mouth.

"I'm glad you think it's so funny. I'd like to see one of you ride on that piece of junk. I can't believe Belterre ever rode it. It belongs in a junkyard!"

Their laughter turned to hysterical hoots. They were pointing at something behind Hannah and laughing so hard they couldn't speak.

Hannah spun around. Belterre was standing in the doorway, smiling.

"Making fun of my good old bike?"

"Uhh, I didn't know you were standing there, Belterre. Um … it's a nice bike. Really." Hannah whirled round to face the other two girls, who were wiping tears of laughter from their eyes. "Why didn't you tell me she was standing there?" she hissed. "Now I've gone and insulted her!"

"That's all right, Hannah honey. I've got a thick skin. It takes a lot more than that to hurt my feelings. But Hannah's right, you know, Maya dear. She's not familiar with these roads like the two of you are. You should let her ride your bike. It will be safer that way. You can ride my beautiful bike, once you clean it up."

This time Maya's eyes grew wide. When she started to splutter, Belterre wagged a finger at her.

"You'll be fine, dear," she said. "Just remember to keep your eye on the road!" Then her face grew suddenly solemn. "And promise you'll stay out of the water."

The ocean was chilly, just as Willie had predicted. As soon as Hannah, Maya and Cassie parked their bikes, they pulled off their socks and sneakers and buried their feet in the warm sand. Then they waded in the cool water, letting it lick their toes and wrap around their ankles.

"It's too cool to swim, like Willie and Belterre said," said Hannah. "I'm not brave enough to go in at this time of year."

"Me neither," said Cassie. "Up to my ankles is far enough. How about you, Maya?"

"No thanks," she said. "I think I'll wait for spring. Let's climb the rocks. We'd better not stick around for too long, though. The tide's coming in and I don't plan on getting wet!"

The girls dashed towards a cluster of rocks that rose high above the surf in a curious collection of tunnels, mountains and caves. The waves crashed against them, spraying a shower of sparkling droplets over the sand and sprinkling their skin with a chilly mist.

"I'm glad I brought a sweatshirt," said Hannah, as she clambered over the rocks. They felt rough and warm against the soles of her feet, as if they still retained some of the heat from the volcano that had deposited them there eons ago. Sitting in the sunshine beside Maya and Cassie, she watched as the tide lapped its way up higher and higher, gulping rocks and swallowing tidepools.

"So does the tide come in at the same time every day or what?" asked Cassie.

Hannah shot a glance at Cassie, just in time to see her being nudged by Maya.

"Of course not," said Maya. "*How long* have you lived here, Cassie? You know it changes every day."

Hannah climbed as high as she could, crouched on a rocky perch and gazed out to sea. The horizon was hazy in the sunshine and there were no boats in sight. *But somewhere out there, far, far across the water and over the land, is my own house and my own room and my own bed*, she thought. Never had everything familiar to her felt so far away. As the seabirds reeled and shrieked over the water, tears prickled her eyes. She quickly blinked them away before Maya and Cassie could notice.

They gobbled the lunch of potted meat sand-wiches, bananas and cookies prepared by Belterre as the wind tousled their hair and the sunshine warmed their backs. Hannah pushed up her sweatshirt sleeves, exposing her winter-white arms, already beginning to show a trace of a tan. Soon, she supposed, she would be brown all year round and sunscreen would become a familiar part of her life. Her mother was always adamant about sunscreen, insistent that she and Jake use it whenever they spent any time on the beach. *But she forgot to remind me today,* thought Hannah. *Too busy house-hunting, of course.*

Chapter Six

On the ride home from the beach, the three girls pedalled their bikes carefully along the winding road overlooking the bay, as small cars and motor scooters zipped by them. Maya and Cassie rode confidently ahead, while Hannah wobbled along behind, her hands clutching the handles in a tight grip, ready to apply the brakes at any moment and cringing each time a vehicle swooped past her in a different direction from the one she was used to in Canada.

The others had just disappeared around a curve when, without warning, a withered old woman stepped out in front of Hannah's lagging bicycle. She squeezed the brakes and veered left, just in time to avoid hitting her, then tumbled head over wheels into a bush hugging the side of the road. As she lay there in a tangle of leaves and branches, trying to catch her breath and decide which way was up, she felt a gentle hand on her shoulder.

When Hannah looked up, a pair of worried brown eyes, deep set in a face as dark and wrinkled as a sun-dried tomato, were peering down at her. Hannah was startled for an instant at the nearness of the woman's face, pushed so close to her own that she could feel warm breath against her skin. She smelled of flowers. Her hair was wrapped in a scarf and her shoulders cloaked with a shawl that wavered in the breeze. She seemed to be shimmering in the afternoon sunshine and Hannah blinked her eyes quickly, thinking they must be playing tricks.

"I'm okay," Hannah reassured her. The woman continued to shimmer, and she blinked again. "I'm wearing a helmet, see," she added, knocking on it. "And I landed in the bushes, so they cushioned my fall. Are you okay?"

The woman's careworn expression remained unchanged.

Hannah stood up and brushed herself off, then started tugging on the bike to free it from the branches lodged in the spokes. At last, she yanked the bike free. "There," she said. "No harm done!"

When she turned to smile at the old woman, she had vanished. Hannah glanced quickly in every direction, but there was no trace of the person she had come so close to knocking over.

"Where the heck did she go?" murmured Hannah, as she climbed back on her bike and began to pedal towards the two girls waiting at a corner up ahead. "That was pretty weird. A person vanishing into thin air."

Maya and Cassie looked puzzled when Hannah breathlessly described what had just happened.

"You're sure you saw someone?" asked Cassie, with a sceptical smile. "You didn't just bang your head and start seeing things or something?"

"Of course not," said Hannah, pointing at her helmet. She frowned when Cassie laughed. "You mean you don't believe me?"

"Sure we believe you, Hannah," said Cassie, then looked over at Maya and twirled her finger in a circle beside her head. "People appear and disappear around here all the time. Right, Maya?"

She thinks I'm nuts, thought Hannah.

Maya nudged Cassie. "It's just that we didn't see anyone and we rode right past the same spot, Hannah," explained Maya. "Maybe it was one of the island ghosts?"

"Yeah, sure." Hannah laughed. "Those are just

folktales that Belterre likes to tell to scare us."

"Island ghosts?" asked Cassie, and Hannah turned to look at her, bewildered.

"Yeah, this island has quite a collection of ghosts," said Maya. "Even though you wouldn't suspect it, what with all the sunshine and blue skies. But they're here, lurking in the shadows, waiting to scare the daylights out of you." Maya shivered and grinned. "How about afternoon tea at the lighthouse and we'll tell you all about some of them. It's just around the corner."

Hannah switched gears as the road began to slope upwards, gliding past Maya, who was struggling to pedal on Belterre's ancient bike. Then she passed Cassie and reached the base of the old lighthouse minutes before the other two girls.

She stood, catching her breath and gazing out at the magnificent ocean view that she'd loved since she was a child. Afternoon tea at the lighthouse had become a tradition during their family vacations in Bermuda.

Why, Hannah wondered, as she watched the turquoise water rippling in the sunshine, did Cassie not know about the multitude of island ghosts? How could you live in Bermuda and not know?

"You don't know about the ghosts, Cassie?" asked Hannah, when they were sitting around a table in the cool, dim lighthouse tearoom. "Belterre used to tell me stories all the time when I was a little kid."

"No doubt about that," said Maya. "She always loved scaring us at bedtime. I used to hear them all the time, too."

Hannah frowned. "So why hasn't Cassie heard any?" she asked.

Cassie glanced over at Maya and Hannah thought she caught a small, secretive smile. "I don't know," she said with a shrug. "I guess I haven't heard as many stories as you two have. We're really not a storytelling family."

Hannah glanced at them both suspiciously. *What are those two conspiring about*, she wondered. Cassie was starting to make her feel uncomfortable with her secret smiles and her teasing ways.

"So how about a story?" said Cassie.

Hunched around the tearoom table, Hannah and Maya told a rapt Cassie about some of the ghosts lurking around the island. In low whispers, they told of a young man's ghost that haunted a dusty road, riding on a motor scooter, old manor houses besieged by spirits from another century, restless spectres of slaves and even ghostly cats. Cassie's tea slowly cooled as she sat wide-eyed, listening. She hadn't taken a single sip, Hannah realised, during the entire storytelling session.

As they wrapped up the last story, Cassie drew a long, deep breath. "Those stories are amazing," she said. "I'm surprised I haven't heard any of them before," she added, winking in Maya's direction.

Hannah squinted suspiciously at both of them, then stared into her teacup.

"Have you thought of the possibility that you actually *did* see a ghost?"

"What?" Hannah almost dropped her glass of juice. "What are you talking about, Maya?"

They were sitting outside on the cedar bench after dinner that night. The winter breeze was cool on Hannah's skin, but nothing like the frigid temperatures they'd be experiencing back home in Canada at this time of year. Sitting in the starry darkness, listening to the distant cries of night birds, Hannah had been caught up in her mixed feelings about Bermuda once again. Until Maya spoke suddenly.

"*Ghosts* is what I'm talking about. Maybe you saw one today. Which would explain the shimmering that you were talking about."

"Okay, I'll agree that I thought I was seeing things when I saw that weird shimmering. But I never thought it could be a ghost! I thought it was the sun playing tricks on me. You don't expect to see a *ghost* in the middle of the day! Why didn't you mention it before?"

"Because I wanted to wait until we were alone," explained Maya. "I didn't want to say anything in front of Cassie, in case she thought we were *both* nuts, instead of just you."

"So she *does* think I'm nuts," said Hannah, letting out a soft sigh. "I had the feeling all day that she doesn't really like me."

"Don't be stupid!" Maya grabbed Hannah's hand and squeezed it. "Of course she likes you. She just has a strange sense of humour. She's a bit sarcastic. You'll get used to it. But I know she doesn't believe in ghosts. That's why I never talk about them in front of her."

"But *you* believe in them? You actually think I might have seen one?"

"Of course I believe. Ghosts are one of my favourite subjects. And you can't believe how jealous I am that you've seen one. I've been waiting for years to see one myself!"

"You have? But why didn't you ever mention it to me?"

"I only see you once a year. And, when you come in the summer, we have other things to do. Besides, most people don't go around blabbing to their friends that they'd like to meet a ghost. It's one of my best-kept secrets."

"But who *was* this person and why did she appear to me? That's what I'd like to know."

"Maybe the best place to start is my grand-mother. Bel has lived here all her life and she knows all about the island. She's so full of stories, she might just know something about your vanishing lady," said Maya.

"Maybe I should describe her to Bel and ask if she knows who it was." Hannah paused and nibbled her lip. "She couldn't have been a ghost, Maya. Why would a ghost appear to *me*, anyway?"

"Oh, they have their reasons," said Maya. "And I think it's a good plan to ask Belterre about her. But maybe you'd better leave out the shimmering part. You don't want my grandmother to think you're nuts, too!"

That night at bedtime, Hannah switched on the lamp beside her bed and unfolded a piece of paper that she'd tucked into her suitcase before leaving Toronto.

Bermuda: good points. Bermuda: bad points. She read each entry out to herself in a quiet voice until she reached *possibly no friends,* with its parade of exclamation marks.

"Possibly no friends," she whispered. "Hmmm." Then she circled the words with a swift slash of her red pen. "I'm not so sure about Cassie. We'll see what happens."

As she turned off her light and rolled over, she thought of the old woman she had seen by the road, about her dark, mournful eyes and that unmistakable scent of flowers. *I know I saw her*, thought Hannah, as she drew the covers up around her chin and snuggled in comfortably. *But, if she really is a ghost, why did she appear to me?*

Chapter Seven

On day two of the Hawthorne family's house-hunting expedition in Bermuda, Hannah awoke at first light. The house was quiet, except for the clatter of kitchen pans that told her Belterre was up and about, preparing food for the rest of the family. Hannah dressed quietly then tiptoed down the hall.

"Good morning," she whispered and Belterre jumped.

"You scared me! I thought I was the only one awake. It's early, dear. Why don't you go back to sleep, at least until that noisy yellow bird wakes you up!"

"I'm not sleepy any more," said Hannah. She sat down at the table, already set for breakfast, and watched as Belterre bustled about the kitchen. "What are you making?"

"A cassava pie," answered Belterre. "We always have it at Christmas. All my grandchildren expect it, even though not all of them like it. It's one of our traditions. I'm going to bake a loquat cake, too, because most everyone likes that."

"I know I do," said Hannah, and had to swallow quickly to stop her mouth from watering. "Can we have some after supper tonight?"

"Of course. I'm making it just for you, Hannah, because I know how much you like it." Belterre pinched Hannah's cheek with a floury hand. "Anything to make my girl happy, you know. Are you happy yet, child?"

"I haven't decided." Hannah brushed away the flour and smiled at her friend. "But I'm trying. I guess I had a nice time yesterday with Maya and Cassie."

"Is that so?" Belterre rinsed and wiped her hands, then sat down at the table across from Hannah. "Tell me about it," she said, as she poured them both a cup of tea.

"Cassie and Maya seem to be such close friends. They get along so well that I feel like an outsider. Maybe when I get to know Cassie better I'll feel more comfortable with her."

Hannah stirred some brown sugar into her tea, then swirled in the milk. "It's weird, though. I seem to know almost as much about the island as she does. I guess because I've been coming here so long. Maya and I told her a bunch of ghost stories."

"And she liked the tales?"

"Of course. Who wouldn't? Oh, and I almost forgot to tell you. I nearly knocked an old woman over on the side of the road yesterday. I crashed Maya's bike in the bushes, too. The woman was okay and so was I, but … " Hannah paused, wondering if Belterre would believe her. "But I turned around to pull my bike out of the tangle and, when I looked back, she was gone. Vanished into thin air. Honest, Bel. I'm not making this up and I didn't imagine it."

Belterre drummed her fingertips on the table. "Hmmm," she said.

"You do believe me, don't you?"

"Of course I do," said Belterre. "I'm trying to figure out who she could be. I know most everyone around here. Was she small and withered? Was her face like an old shoe?"

"An old shoe?" Hannah giggled. "I suppose

so. But she had kind eyes and she smelt like flowers."

"Strange," said Belterre, wrinkling up her nose the way she often did when she was thinking hard. "What was she wearing?"

"Wearing? Let's see … there was some sort of scarf thingy on her head and a shawl was wrapped around her shoulders. I'm not sure what her dress was like, though. I didn't get a chance to look at her long enough!"

"My gosh," murmured Belterre softly, as she stroked her chin. Hannah was sure she saw her eyes well up with tears before she quickly blinked them away.

"What is it, Bel? What's wrong?"

"Old Martha Cox. I haven't seen her in years." Bel's voice had grown hoarse and she clutched her throat. "Thought she was gone for good. I wonder what brought her out yesterday?"

Hannah frowned. "Why? Is she some kind of hermit or something? Why doesn't she ever come out?"

"Because she's dead, dear," said Belterre with a shrug.

"Dead!" Hannah jumped to her feet, knocking

back her chair, which hit the floor with a clatter. "How can she be dead? I *saw* her, Bel. As plain as I'm seeing you right now. She even touched me. On my arm."

"What you saw," said Belterre, patting Hannah's hand gently, "was the *ghost* of Martha Cox." When Hannah's whole body shivered, Bel clucked her tongue. "Don't be alarmed. I saw her myself, many times, but that was more than twenty years ago. When I was going through a sad time in my life. When Celia was leaving the island. So I suppose those are the people who see her. People who are going through troubled times. Because … " Bel paused and sighed deeply. "Because of poor Martha's own tragic life."

Hannah stared at Belterre as she slowly sat back down. "But when did she die?" she whispered.

"Oh, about thirty years ago," said Bel. "She just fell down and died one day, right on the spot where you saw her. And now they say she's watching out for others there. Some say she warns people. Tries to stop the same thing from happening to them. Most don't see her, though. Only people with troubles, as I said before."

"You're telling me I saw a ghost?"

"This island is cluttered up with ghosts. You know that, Hannah. It has such a rich history, with pirates and shipwrecks and slaves and settlers, there's bound to be lots of sorrowful spirits left behind. I used to tell you all those tales, remember?"

"Sure," said Hannah. "But that's just what I thought they were. Tales. Tall ones. I didn't think they could possibly be true. When I curled up in a ball under my covers at night, scared to fall asleep, I'd try to convince myself that you were making it all up, just to entertain me."

Belterre chuckled softly. "I'm so sorry, child. I didn't know I was scaring you so much. You should have told me to stop."

"But I *liked* the stories, Bel. That's why I asked to hear them over and over again. Everyone likes ghost stories. But actually meeting a ghost. Something tells me I'll have trouble falling asleep tonight."

"Martha is a kindly soul. Nothing to be afraid of, Hannah. I'm just surprised that she popped in after all these years. Maybe she sensed your troubles and she was trying to comfort you.

Because she had so many troubles of her own, you see."

"Troubles? What sort of troubles, Bel?"

Bel's eyes filled again.

"Bel?" Hannah frowned. Tears in Belterre's eyes were a rare sight. "What kind of troubles?"

Belterre quickly dabbed at her eyes with her apron. "Oh, Hannah. It was so long ago. It's just too hard to recollect right now."

"Did you know her?" asked Hannah, puzzled by the forlorn look on Belterre's face, the way her eyes looked lost and distant, as if she were gazing into the past.

"I knew *of* her," said Bel, "and I know how she suffered."

"The poor thing." Hannah shook her head sadly. "It's too bad her spirit can't rest in peace. But she sure helped to distract me, because now I won't be able to stop thinking about her."

"What's all the racket?" Jake was standing in the doorway, squinting. "It's hardly even light out yet. Why are you making so much noise?"

"Oh, we're just sharing ghost stories," said Hannah.

Jake eagerly pulled up a chair. "But I like

hearing ghost stories, too. How about sharing some of them with me?"

"Okay," agreed Hannah with a wide grin. "And have I got a good one for you! Brace yourself for a shiver, kiddo!"

Belterre's face was still solemn. "Maybe you shouldn't, Hannah," she murmured. "You might scare him. He's only twelve. Why don't you just forget about it?"

"No way." Jake thumped on the table with his fist. "Let's hear it, Banana."

As Hannah helped Belterre prepare the porridge and finish her baking, she told Jake the whole story. He slouched at the table, his sleepy eyes slowly growing wider and more alert, his back straightening up as the tale progressed. Soon his jaw had begun to drop until his mouth was hanging open in astonishment.

"You're telling me you actually met a ghost?" said Jake, as Bel ladled porridge into a couple of bowls for them. "Wow! That's so cool! I wish I could meet her. Do you think if I hang around the lighthouse that I might run into her, too?"

Hannah frowned as she sprinkled brown sugar on to the hot oats. "Not likely. Bel said that she usually appears to troubled people and you never seem to have any troubles."

"But you will," Bel warned him with a wink, "if you don't finish every single bite of that porridge. Eat up now, my boy. Don't let it get cold!"

When Bel glanced at Hannah for an instant before turning back to the kitchen sink, Hannah was sure she saw something in her friend's familiar face that she'd never seen before. Almost as if the sparkle had gone out of her eyes.

Chapter Eight

Jake couldn't stop talking about the ghost of Martha Cox. He was yapping about her so much that Hannah was almost sorry she'd related her spooky escapade to him in the first place. And their mother was just sitting there, smiling and nodding patiently as she listened to the story over and over again.

All the way to the ferry wharf in Willie's taxi, and now, seated on the ferry crossing the harbour to Hamilton, his mouth just wouldn't stay shut. Willie had offered to drive them right into the city, but Jake had insisted on the traditional ferry ride he liked so much.

Sitting beside him, listening to his constant babbling, Hannah was sure it was going to take forever. She was almost tempted to put her hand over his mouth to keep him quiet for a while. When Jake stopped talking for a moment to catch his breath, their mother took off her sunglasses and squinted at them in the sunshine.

"It's sounds like you two are having fun," she said, gazing off across the harbour. "And maybe Dad and I will be able to relax for a few days, too. Because I think we've already found a place to live."

Hannah felt her heart starting to bounce around in her chest.

"Really," she said, trying her best to smile and look interested. "Whereabouts?"

"Well, it's just outside of Hamilton, nice and close to the bank where Dad is going to work. In fact, he could probably walk there each day. And you two will be close to the school."

"What's it like? Will I have a big bedroom?" Jake was squirming in his seat, a huge smile splitting his freckled face.

"You sure will," said Mum, getting into the spirit of Jake's excitement. "And guess what? It even has a pool! And a den and a fireplace."

"A pool? Did you say a pool? Let's move in right now!"

Mum laughed and ruffled Jake's sandy hair. "I think we'd better go home to Toronto and pack first," she said. Then she glanced over at Hannah.

Hannah looked down at her lap. She didn't want her mother to notice the tears that had welled up in her eyes, the ones that she was desperately trying to blink away before they could trickle down her cheek.

"That's great, Mum," she said.

"Do you really think so, Hannah?" Her mum reached out a cool hand and stroked the tight knot of fingers entwined on Hannah's lap. "Do I still have to try to convince you that this is a good thing, a good experience for a girl your age?"

"No. You don't have to try to convince me," said Hannah. "I just have to get used to the idea, that's all. Maybe after I see the house … "

"Terrific. Because we're meeting Dad there in half an hour. You can check the place out, see how you like it. I'd like you and Jake to help us make the decision."

"But I thought we were going shopping," said Hannah, desperately trying to come up with an excuse to delay the inevitable.

"We'll do that after lunch, Hannah," replied Mum in a soothing voice. "But let's have a look at the house first. Okay?"

Hannah nodded slowly.

"I get first dibs on a bedroom." Jake yelled so loudly that some of the other passengers spun around to stare at him.

They caught a taxi at the ferry dock in Hamilton and were whisked within minutes to the house chosen by their parents – a pastel pink bungalow with glossy black shutters, built of sturdy limestone. The house was surrounded by flowering shrubs and lush palms.

"I never thought I'd live in a marshmallow pink house with palm trees in the garden," said Hannah as she stepped from the cab.

"I can see a slide! The pool has a slide!" hooted Jake, bolting straight for the low wall that surrounded the back garden to get a better look.

Their dad was already there. He came loping out of the house with the estate agent, his face alight with a joyful, boyish smile. He looked just like Jake, Hannah thought, grinning from ear to ear like that, his sandy hair tousled by the wind. Seeing the excitement on his face, she felt a slow, uncertain smile creep over her own. Dad's enthusiasm was always infectious. And, from the outside, the bungalow did look amazing.

Jake dashed back from his pool inspection in time to get through the doorway ahead of everyone else and soon had his bedroom picked out.

"This one's mine!" he declared, as Hannah came down the hall. "It has doors that go out to the pool!"

"Sorry, pal, but this is the master bedroom," said Dad, sympathetically patting Jake on the shoulder. "It has the ensuite bathroom, too. You'll have to share the other bathroom with Hannah. And I'm afraid you'll have to use the kitchen door to get out to the pool."

The other two bedrooms were so similar that Jake gave Hannah first choice. "Maybe you should have the one closest to the bathroom, since you always spend so much time in there. And I'll have the one closest to the kitchen … and the fridge. What do you think, Hannah?"

"Sounds fine, I guess," said Hannah.

She walked slowly from room to room, listening to the low murmur of her parents discussing their plans with the estate agent out in the courtyard. She tried to imagine herself living in the house, doing her homework at a table in the bright kitchen, curling up to sleep in the cosy bedroom, sitting by a fire in the den, reading a book or watching television. Bringing new friends home? It all seemed so unbelievable and strange that in a couple of months this unfamiliar place would be her home.

At lunchtime, the Hawthorne family sat out on the balcony of a restaurant on Front Street and gazed down at the hustle and bustle of traffic on the street. The whizzing cars, scooters and taxis, the steady stream of strolling pedestrians, the clop and squeak of horse-drawn carriages wheeling through the streets with their cargo of camera-laden tourists – it all became a jumbled blur as Hannah munched slowly on her fish and chips and tried to get used to the idea of becoming a temporary citizen of Bermuda. She wondered if she ever would.

At least Jake had stopped talking about Martha Cox after being distracted by the new pink house and the shopping expedition. But he didn't stop talking about ghosts for very long. During their visit to the children's bookshop, Jake bought as many books about ghosts and hauntings as his mother would allow.

"I think three is plenty, Jake," she told him as they left the shop. "That's enough reading material to last for a little while, anyway. Consider it an early Christmas present."

"Thanks, Mum," said Jake, grinning as he clutched his precious bag.

"I just hope you'll be able to sleep tonight after filling your head with all those spooky tales. Please don't come wandering into our room in the middle of the night, complaining about scary dreams," Dad warned him.

"Don't worry, Dad, I won't. Which book did you get, Hannah?"

"The next book in the Narnia series that I'm reading," said Hannah. "You can read it after me if you want. And maybe I can have a look at yours."

It was a much quieter trip home to Belterre's place in the taxi late that afternoon. Jake had his face buried in ghost stories, her parents murmured on about moving plans and Hannah gazed out the window at the sunshine-bright scenery. It seemed so strange to see houses festively decorated with wreaths, ribbons and garlands for Christmas in such a summery climate.

On the taxi radio, the local station played a constant stream of holiday songs about Santa, Jack Frost and sleigh bells ringing in the snow that just didn't seem to match the balmy weather. All the shop windows in Hamilton were festooned with Christmas trees, snowmen and fake snow, while shoppers strolled past in shorts and sandals. *It all seems so weird, so unreal,* thought Hannah. *Thank goodness we're spending Christmas at home, where everything makes sense and there actually is some snow on the ground!*

As the taxi passed the Lighthouse Road, Jake let out a sudden yelp that startled all of them.

"Stop the taxi. I want to get out and walk home from here!"

"Please pull over." Dad signalled the driver with a light tap on the shoulder. "Why do you want to get out now, Jake? It's a bit of a hike yet from here over to Bel and Willie's place. And there's a lot of traffic right now, so you'll have to be careful."

"I know why you want to get out," Hannah muttered near his ear. "But you'll never see Martha Cox. She only appears to troubled people."

"Want to bet?" said Jake. He already had the door open and was clambering out.

"Now, Jake, I'm not so sure about this … " began Mum.

"I'll walk back with him," blurted Hannah, even though she was tired from walking around town and her feet hurt in the new sandals she was wearing. She would have liked nothing more than to sit on the old cedar bench and sip a cold drink back at Belterre's. But an odd, nagging thought nudged her out of the taxi behind Jake.

Chapter Nine

What was it that Belterre had told her? *Some say she warns people. Tries to stop the same thing from happening to them.* For some reason, those words had been etched into Hannah's head like words carved into marble.

There were no walkways along the winding road and Hannah kept a tight grip on Jake's T-shirt as he walked ahead of her, wincing each time a vehicle whizzed past, dangerously close.

"Why on earth did they let you get out here?" fumed Hannah, as she steered her brother away from the oncoming traffic. "This is crazy. You're not going to see any ghost."

"I'm not looking for a ghost. Let go of me, Banana!" Jake tried to tug himself free. "Why did you get out of the taxi if you didn't want to? I don't need babysitting, you know!"

"You think you're some stupid ghost-hunter or something, now that you've got those books. I know how your mind works, Jake. I *know* you're looking for Martha Cox. But I'm telling you, she won't be there. WILL YOU JUST LISTEN TO ME!" Hannah grabbed hold of his shoulder and spun him around. "This is the spot. Right here where we're standing. Tell me. Do you see any ghosts?"

"This is it? This is the spot?" Jake looked around casually enough, but Hannah could tell he was nervous by the way his nose was twitching. "This is where you dumped your bike?"

"Right in these bushes," said Hannah, pointing to the tangle by the road. "And Martha Cox was standing right there."

"Right here?" Jake gazed hopefully at the spot, as if he expected Martha Cox to materialise from nowhere, just the way she'd vanished. "Cool," he whispered. "Let's wait around a bit and see if she shows up. Martha? Are you here, Martha Cox?"

"Jake, you fool. Can't you understand … " Hannah swallowed back the furious words that jumped into her mind and took a deep breath before she continued. "She's not here. You can't just expect her to show up on demand. She's not a sideshow exhibit, you know!"

"And she's not *your* ghost, either," said Jake. "Just because you saw her first, doesn't mean you own her. Anyone can look for her if they want to. Including me. And if I want to look for Martha Cox, then I will."

"That's it!" Hannah's voice was growing shrill. "We're going home right now. You're not making any sense at all, Jake. All of a sudden you're obsessed with ghosts." She gripped her brother by the elbow and prodded him in the direction of the side road that led to Belterre and Willie's place.

"I'm not going!" He tried to squirm from her grip. "You can't make me. Hah," he yelled triumphantly, wrenching his arm from her fingers. "I'll do what I like!" Then he leaped out of reach – and stumbled right on to the busy road!

For an instant, Hannah froze, watching in morbid horror, knowing there wasn't a thing she could do to prevent this tragedy from playing itself out before her eyes, as if she'd been forcibly dragged into the plot of a terrifying movie.

Then something beyond the confusing blur of swerving vehicles and din of honking horns jolted her into action. Something like an uncanny shove from behind that nearly knocked her off balance and sent her reeling in the direction of her brother, who lay crumpled like a rag doll on the road in front of the oncoming traffic.

A sudden rush of power raced through her limbs and propelled her forwards to drag him out of the way. Seconds later, a taxi stopped dead with a loud screech of tyres, right in the spot where Jake had just been lying. The driver hit the horn, jarring Jake out of his frightened daze, and then pulled the car over to the side of the road, out of the way of the traffic. The door burst open and Willie jumped out.

"What are you two doing here?" Willie's usually gentle voice was shaking with anger. "Why are you playing by the road? I almost hit the boy! I almost hit our Jake!"

Jake was standing up by the roadside now, his eyes wide and terrified as the stream of traffic picked up again and flowed swiftly past them as if nothing had happened. He had started to shiver.

"I'm sorry, Willie," he said. "I tripped. I didn't mean to fall on the road."

"Well I should hope not!" Willie began to chuckle softly, his anger melting away as he placed his hands on Jake's shoulders and looked him in the eye. "I'm so glad that nothing happened. I'm sorry I shouted, but I almost hit you. I'm not even going to ask why you two are walking along this road. It's a blind curve, you know. The oncoming traffic can't see you until it's right on top of you. Like I almost was! Get in the car, kids. Let's go home."

"Thanks, Willie," said Hannah, and hugged his arm just before she climbed into the back seat of the van.

In the few minutes that it took to reach Willie and Belterre's house, a whirlwind of thoughts spun through Hannah's head, always followed by Belterre's prophetic words. *Some say she warns people. Tries to stop the same thing from happening to them.* Something had pushed Hannah from behind when Jake fell on the road. A strange force that she couldn't quite identify. She'd heard of people having a sudden rush of adrenalin in emergency situations that propelled them to take action or perform incredible feats. Had it simply been a rush of adrenalin that had spurred her on? Or had it been something more, a supernatural force? *Some say she warns people.* Could it have been Martha Cox who pushed her, who urged her to save her brother?

"It couldn't have been," murmured Hannah.

"Couldn't have been what?" asked Jake. He was grinning at her, apparently completely recovered. A tiny trickle of dried blood on his knee was now the only sign of his mishap. "Couldn't have been what, Hannah?"

"Nothing, Jake. Absolutely nothing."

But, if it had been absolutely nothing, why had she detected the unmistakable scent of flowers just as she climbed into the taxi?

Later that day, while Jake watched a chequers competition between Dad and Willie, and Mum helped Belterre with dinner preparations, Hannah snatched her brother's ghost books from the shelf beside his bed and sneaked outside with them. Curled up on the cedar bench, sipping her longed-for cold drink, she flipped slowly through the pages, goose bumps prickling on her arms as spooky apparitions flitted through her imagination.

One book in particular was filled with tales of Bermuda ghosts. There was nothing about Martha Cox, but the rest of the stories were both eerie and fascinating. She recognised the tale of the ghost on the motor scooter, and some of the others that Bel had related to her long ago, especially a favourite about a ghost that liked to hide things from homeowners and knock over shelves of glass and crystal ornaments. She also recognised tales about ringing bells on a deserted road, apparitions of cats and dogs, the clop of an invisible horse's hooves and encounters with long-dead slaves, chains still attached to their ankles.

But, when she discovered several references to the scent of perfume or flowers during ghostly encounters, Hannah found herself shivering in the late afternoon heat.

"Most of all I remember her smell. It was the sweet smell of a cleanly washed woman. It was not perfumed and, somehow, it was reassuring and familiar." (Page 56, *Bermuda's Favourite Haunts.*)

Hannah read the lines twice, then peered nervously over her shoulder. "I'm scaring myself," she murmured. "I'm the one who won't be able to sleep tonight."

But Hannah could not shake the weird experience from her mind. She couldn't banish the sight of Jake lying on the road and the feeling of a shove from behind, something spurring her to take action, something that was more than adrenalin. She couldn't forget the flowery scent that had filled her nostrils, either. Even when she closed the books and gazed out over the bay at the ruffled whitecaps, at the gulls that tipped and reeled in the breeze, even when she inhaled the fresh ocean air, she couldn't forget.

When she finally dozed off in the shade, the bothersome thoughts had finally started to melt away like a snowman on a sunny day. She relaxed in the stillness of the warm afternoon, felt the shivers of uneasiness slowly trickling from her body – until something grabbed her from behind.

Hannah shrieked and leaped to her feet. Maya was grinning at her, wide-eyed, as she leaned over the bench.

"Maya! You shouldn't sneak up on people like that! You scared me half to death! What's the matter with you?"

"I always sneak up from behind and scare you when you're sitting on this bench. It's tradition. And you always laugh after you scream. So what's the matter with *you*?"

Hannah sat down and patted the bench. "Did Cassie come with you?" she asked, as Maya sat down beside her.

"Yeah. She's inside, playing chequers with Jake. She thinks he's cute!"

"Cute!" Hannah groaned. "A girl thinks my goofy brother is cute? Yuk! Well, I'm glad you came out here alone, Papaya, because I've got a tale to share."

Chapter Ten

By the time Hannah reached the part when Willie almost ran Jake over with his taxi, Maya was perched on the edge of her seat and her wide smile had all but withered away.

"Hannah, that's incredible," she whispered. "And I was right. It really was a ghost! Do you know how many ghosts I've heard about on this island? Do you know how long I've wanted to see one? And you met one in the middle of the day! Right by the side of the road! No wonder you looked so funny when you came riding up to Cassie and me on the bike. My hair would have been standing straight up!"

"Well, the hair on my arms sure was," said Hannah. "I had more goose bumps than a goose!"

Maya drummed her fingers on her knees for a moment before she spoke again. "We've got to find out more about Martha Cox. They say that sometimes ghosts have unfinished business that keeps them stuck here on earth. So what can hers be? Why won't she move on to the other side?"

"Belterre didn't say anything about that," said Hannah.

"I can't understand why I've never heard the story of Martha Cox before, though," continued Maya. "Why didn't Belterre ever tell me?"

Hannah paused. "Well … for some reason she wasn't too thrilled about discussing Martha Cox. She got this funny look on her face and her eyes teared up. She said that she hadn't thought about Martha in years. Maybe that's why she never told you about her. It seemed to me like it was something she was trying to forget."

"Why would she be trying to forget?" Maya tugged pensively at one of the little knots of hair on her head. "Who *was* this Martha Cox?"

"I'm not sure, but Bel said that she's been dead for thirty years. Oh, and that she had all sorts of troubles in her life. And tragedies."

"Ahhh." Maya nodded. "That's what's keeping her anchored to earth. Something that happened in the past. Something that's still bothering her."

"And how can we find out what that is?"

"That's a good question. Whenever I need information, I usually head for the library over on Queen Street in Hamilton. They have tons of information about Bermuda. Maybe we can find out more about Martha Cox over there, in the archives or in old newspapers."

"That's a great idea," agreed Hannah. "Maybe we can learn something about where she lived and how she died. Let's go right now!"

"We can't. The library closes at six o'clock. It's nearly four now. We'd never have enough time to get over there and do all that research. How about I pick you up on my scooter tomorrow morning at ten?"

"Perfect," said Hannah. "This is so cool. I never thought I'd be ghost-hunting in Bermuda. I hope we have enough time to find out something about Martha Cox before I have to go home in three days. Maybe we can stay a bit longer."

"Funny," said Maya with a crooked grin. "A couple of days ago you didn't want to be here at all and now you want to stay longer?"

"Hmmm," murmured Hannah, and pensively chewed her lip.

Maya and Cassie stayed for supper. There were tuna steaks and cassava pie and loquat cake for dessert, just as Belterre had promised. Jake sat beside Cassie, his new-found fan, and yammered on about the new house and his bedroom and the pool with the slide that he couldn't wait to try. He talked about the restaurant balcony where they'd eaten and about the three ghost books that Mum had bought him at the children's bookshop, even inviting Cassie to borrow them.

Jake also mentioned what a coincidence it was that Willie had been driving past and picked the two of them up by the side of the road when they were walking home. But he never said a thing about the mishap near the lighthouse and, when his eyes met Hannah's in an unspoken pledge of silence, they both glanced uncomfortably over at Willie. But he was munching quietly on his dessert and, to their relief, never added another word to the conversation.

They divided into teams to play chequers after supper. Of course, Jake was Cassie's partner and the two of them beat all the other teams.

"Wow! What a team we make!" Cassie gave Jake a high five and Hannah was sure she saw him blushing. "Do you want to hang out tomorrow, Jake? Maya and Hannah are going into Hamilton and there's only room for two on the scooter."

Jake glanced over at his parents for approval and they both nodded.

"Sure!" Jake said. "Maybe we can play chequers, then go for a bike ride or something."

"Sounds good to me," Cassie said. "I'll even let you ride my mountain bike."

That night Hannah's head met the pillow much earlier than usual. She tried to read her new Narnia book for a while, but her heavy eyelids kept fluttering shut, and she found herself reading the same paragraph over and over again. Finally she gave up and flicked out the light beside her bed. Darkness fell and it was a few moments before her eyes had adjusted.

Soon pinpoints of starlight appeared outside the bedroom window as she wavered between wakefulness and sleep. She could hear the faint lapping of waves along the shore and the distant shrieks of night birds, until the curtain of sleep finally closed over her.

Hannah's dreams were strange and whispery that night. Ghosts flitted through them as they flitted through the pages of the books she had been reading earlier in the day – ghosts that barked and meowed, ghosts that drove cars and peered through mirrors, ghosts that threw objects at her and laughed. She would awaken now and then, snuggle up in a tight ball and bury herself under the covers until a restless slumber washed over her once more.

During the last dream, though, Hannah sat up in bed and gasped. Her skin was sweaty and shivery at the same time and her heart was playing a rapid drumbeat in her chest. She was sure she had seen her, standing there beside her bed. Clad in a shawl, with a scarf knotted around her head. Leaning close, breathing on Hannah's face. Smelling like flowers. Touching her arm gently, reassuringly.

"Martha," she whispered into the night. But her words were swallowed up by the unchanging darkness. "Too many ghost stories yesterday," she told herself, before tossing and turning the rest of the night until dawn peeked through her window.

Hannah adjusted her helmet, then clung to Maya's waist, screwing up her eyes against the rushing air as the motor scooter picked up speed along the winding road to Hamilton. She wasn't really nervous – Maya was a careful driver and the speed limit was low. But the same thrill filled her body every time Maya took her for a ride. To be zipping along in the open air, gazing out at the wide ocean vistas and nodding palms as the wind blew in her face! It made her feel so much more independent and free than she ever did back home. In Toronto, nobody drove small motor scooters like they did here in Bermuda. Too dangerous, her father always said. Too many crazy, impatient drivers.

When they reached the busy streets of Hamilton, Santa drove up beside them in a fire truck and waved at Hannah. *How about that*, she thought. *Up north in Canada, Santa usually rides in a sleigh.* Then the traffic was held up by a troupe of Bermuda's traditional Gombey dancers in bright, bizarre costumes, dancing across the road to the throb of drums and the shrill shriek of whistles, vanishing just as quickly as they had appeared.

"Don't get to see them very often," shouted Maya over her shoulder.

"It's my first time," Hannah shouted back over the whine of the motor. "They don't come out very often, do they?"

Maya shook her head and drove on.

They parked near the library and walked over in the sunshine. The pavements bustled with chattering, parcel-laden shoppers and Christmas music seeped from every store. But inside the library it was dim and cool and wonderfully quiet. Maya steered Hannah directly to the reference section.

"Our hunt begins right here," she said. "We're searching for any reference we can find to Martha Cox. What we need is microfilm of newspapers from thirty years ago. At least we can find out when and how she died. Do you have any idea what year it was, Hannah?"

"Afraid not," admitted Hannah. "I'm not a very good detective, am I? Bel never mentioned the year and she looked so sad that I didn't want to ask her any more questions."

"That's okay. We'll start with a newspaper from thirty years ago. If we don't find her in there, you can look at the death notices for the following years and I'll look at the preceding years. Does that make sense?"

"Sounds almost organised," said Hannah. "I can hardly wait to start."

It was slow going, even after the librarian had set them up with the microfilm and showed them how to search for the information they were seeking.

"This is taking forever," groaned Maya, after two hours of searching had turned up nothing. "I'm starting to wonder if this woman ever existed. And I'm getting hungry, too. What about stopping for lunch, Hannah?"

"Not yet," said Hannah in a determined voice. "Who knows, I might find her on the very next page that I check. And so might you. So keep looking!"

"Yes, Captain," said Maya, with a brisk, ironic salute. "But my neck's getting stiff and my stomach is grumbling and growling so loud that people are starting to stare. The hunger monster that lives in my belly is complaining that it's been too long since breakfast!"

"Hang on a minute, Maya. Just a minute. I think I've found something here. Listen to this: *Cox, Martha Jane, of Southampton Parish, passed away suddenly on October 17. She left no family as her two sons, Samuel and Robert, and her husband, Albert, had died before her.*

"Maya, I think we finally found her!"

Chapter Eleven

Their heads pressed together, Maya and Hannah read in silence about the "homegoing services" for Martha Cox. Services had been held in a church in Southampton Parish, the funeral notice said, and it concluded with a brief paragraph:

A sad end to a tragic life. Martha Cox never overcame the grief of losing her two young boys to the sea years ago. Their bodies were never found. May your soul rest in peace, Martha, in this final reunion with your loved ones.

"She was sixty-five years old when she passed on," said Maya. "And her children and husband all died before her. She must have lived a sad life, with all her loved ones gone. It must have been horrible, losing her little boys like that."

"Belterre never said anything about those

boys." Hannah tapped her fingers on the desk. "I wonder why."

"Maybe she thought you would be upset by it," suggested Maya.

"But it happened ages ago. Why would I be upset over something that happened so far back, when I'd never even heard of Martha Cox until yesterday? You know what, Maya? I think Belterre was the one who was upset and didn't want to discuss it. She clammed up about it pretty fast so I wouldn't ask any more questions. Sort of brushed the whole thing off and changed the subject."

"But why?" Maya tugged thoughtfully on a knot of hair and scanned the obituary once more. "What does any of this have to do with my grandmother?"

"Wait a minute," said Hannah. Her fingertips began to drum urgently on the desk. "There must have been an article in the newspaper sixty years ago when the little boys were drowned. Maya, let's check back sixty years."

"Ohhh no!" Maya stood up and started to tug on her windbreaker. "I'm not bending over this desk for one more second. Not until I feed the monsters that are howling in my stomach. Let's go, Hannah. I know a nice little deli where we can grab a sandwich."

Outside once more, blinking in the bright sunshine, Hannah realised that her stomach was grumbling for some lunch as well. As they stood waiting in line to order sandwiches at the deli, she looked around uncomfortably, hoping that nobody would notice.

"Sounds like a couple of puppies are having a fight under your jacket," said Maya, her eyes twinkling. "You must be even hungrier than I am."

Hannah rolled her eyes. "I was so caught up in Martha's story, I didn't even notice," she said. "But just the smell in here is driving me crazy. I'm dying for a chicken salad sandwich."

"Roast beef for me," said Maya. "And thank goodness we're next in line. I'm about ready to jump right over the counter and make *my own* sandwich!"

They lounged on a bench in Point Pleasant Park, munching thick sandwiches and sipping sodas while they gazed off across Hamilton Harbour.

As they watched, the ferry arrived and spilled its cargo on to the dock. Passengers streamed in every direction; tourists slung with cameras, agog at all the new sights, businessmen in the Bermuda "uniform" of shorts, knee socks and blazers, glancing at their watches as they hurried off to keep appointments, young mothers pushing babies in strollers, tight knots of chattering teenagers. Then a new load of passengers flowed up the gangplank and soon the ferry steamed away.

It really is a pretty place, Hannah couldn't help but think, as she watched the buzz of activity. The girls swallowed the last of their sandwiches, threw their lunch litter into a nearby waste basket and headed back to the library in the mid-afternoon sunshine.

By four o'clock, Hannah was tired and frustrated. After two more hours of examining dozens of old newspapers on the microfilm, she felt as though the Gombeys were dancing in her head and they hadn't found a trace of information about the tragic deaths of the two Cox boys.

"I've had it," sighed Maya. "I think we need more details about when those kids died or we'll be searching through these old newspapers forever."

"But where will we find *that* information? I

wouldn't even know where to begin to look or who to ask. Anyone who would recall the story must be pretty old by now. They'd probably have forgotten all the important details." Hannah shook her head. "I think we're on a wild goose chase here, Maya. I'm about ready to give up. I'm going home to Canada soon. We'll never have enough time."

"Never say never," Maya told her sternly. "We'll think of something. There must be *someone* on this island who knows this story!"

"Well, it would have to be someone old, that's for sure," Hannah reminded her.

"Hmm. Someone old." Maya squinted thoughtfully. "I'll ask around," she said. "Let's head for home now, Banana."

By the time Hannah was dropped off, dinner preparations were well under way. Belterre shooed her out of the kitchen because she'd already recruited Jake as a helper. With a glass of chilled papaya juice in her hand, Hannah settled herself in her favourite spot on the cedar bench to think.

She and Maya had learned a little about

Martha Cox today, but it wasn't very much to go on. They knew when she'd died and how tragic a life she'd lived. Still, it wasn't enough information to explain why Martha's ghost was still hanging around, breathing on Hannah's face, pushing her from behind and staring at her with those sad dark eyes. Or why just the mention of her name could bring tears to Belterre's eyes.

"Martha's trying to tell me something," Hannah murmured to herself. "I just know she is."

Hannah made up her mind, then and there. It was her turn to help with the dinner dishes. And, somehow, she planned to bring up the name of Martha Cox again, to tell Belterre what she and Maya had learned about the dead woman's life, to learn even more, if she could. She only hoped that her questions wouldn't make Bel cry again.

Hannah was nervous all through dinner, but luckily Jake did so much chattering about his bike ride to the lighthouse with Cassie that no one paid much attention to her. *At least she gets along with one of us*, Hannah caught herself thinking.

Mum and Dad seemed to find it charming that Jake had had a "first date" of sorts and Willie kept teasing him about the "first kiss", which Jake didn't appreciate. Even Hannah felt sorry for him when she saw him squirming in his seat. Only Belterre was quieter than usual, and now and then Hannah would cast a sly glance in her direction, only to see her staring intently into her plate.

Her mother did ask why she had so little food on her own plate and Hannah explained that she and Maya had eaten a late lunch. She kept trying to make a joke out of it, telling everyone that she was saving her portion for Dad, because of his famous Bermuda appetite. It made them laugh and helped to distract them from her nervousness.

At last, Hannah and Belterre were alone in the kitchen. Hannah was just about to open her mouth and let the first words slip out when Bel beat her to it.

"Something's wrong," she said as she filled the sink with water.

"What do you mean?" Hannah asked, twisting the dish towel in her hands. Her voice was a whispery squeak. Bel spun around to look at her.

"You can't fool me, Hannah Hawthorne. I know you well enough by now. Something is bothering you and it isn't the move to Bermuda any more. I can see it in your eyes. They're all jumpy and your face looks fretful. Is it because of that Martha Cox story?"

Hannah's eyes grew wide and her fretful face sagged with disbelief. "You can read me like a book, can't you, Bel?"

"That's right," said Bel. "But I can't read between the lines. Why is Martha on your mind?" There were no tears in Bel's dark eyes, now fixed unblinkingly on Hannah. But Hannah could see that her forehead was creased with concern.

"Well … " Hannah began carefully. "Maya and I found out a little more about her today."

"And how did you do that?" Dishes clattered as Belterre turned back to the sink and began scrubbing the plates in the soapy water.

"We went to the library, Bel. Maya and I. We looked for Martha's obituary in old newspapers."

"You mean to tell me they have newspapers sitting around at the library from so long ago?"

"They're all saved on microfilm," explained

Hannah. "Anyway, we found the right one and now we know when Martha Cox died."

"Why are you so interested in that? It's only a ghost story, dear. It might not even be a true one." Bel handed Hannah a dripping plate. "Why don't you just forget all about it, pretend it never happened?"

As she reached for the plate, Hannah caught Bel's strange sidelong glance, the peculiar look in her eye, the quick blinking, as if something were making her uncomfortable.

"Because I *saw* her, Bel. I've seen her a couple of times. She's a restless spirit, and something is keeping her here on Earth."

"Now who filled your head with such nonsense, Hannah? Was it Maya? I know she loves all this haunting and ghosts. Is it her who's got you convinced that Martha Cox is stuck on Earth?" Now Belterre wouldn't even look at Hannah as she rattled on. "I told you before and I'll tell you again. This island is cluttered up with ghosts. Just about everyone says they've seen one. But it doesn't mean all the stories are true."

"But you told me you saw Martha's ghost yourself, years ago," Hannah reminded her.

"When you were going through some troubling times. Just the other day you told me that. You said she's watching out for other people."

"Did I?" Belterre continued to stare into the sink as if something fascinating lurked in the sudsy water. "I can't seem to remember that. So tell me, what are you hoping to find under the Christmas tree this year, honey?"

As Belterre changed the subject, Hannah was sure she saw a couple of tears slip from her face and into the dishwater that she seemed to find so absorbing.

When the dishes were done, the whole family gathered in the cosy living room, reminiscing about old times while Willie and Jake competed in their ongoing chequers tournament. The phone rang and Belterre answered.

"You'd like to speak to whom?" she said. "I'm sorry. I can't hear you very well. Who is this, please?"

Belterre's eyes flicked uneasily around the room as she listened to the voice on the other end of the line. "Pardon me. Could you repeat that, please," she said again, turning her face towards the wall. "Who is it you want?"

There was a pause, then, "No, I'm sorry," Hannah heard her say. "There's nobody here by that name. Yes. You're welcome. Goodbye now."

"Who was it?" Jake asked. "Who did they want to speak to, Bel?"

"It was Santa Claus," said Bel. "He wanted to speak to one of the elves!" When everyone in the room laughed at her joke, she turned her gaze towards Hannah. Bel's wide smile was belied by the discomfort in her eyes. Hannah looked down at her knees, focusing on her hands, tightly knotted on her lap.

"Would anyone like something to drink?" asked Bel brightly, as she whisked towards the kitchen amid a chorus of *Yes please*. "I'm very thirsty myself. Must have been that salty chowder. I'm sure I added too much salt this time."

Hannah watched her back disappear into the next room, then looked down at her hands once again. For some reason she had a feeling that phone call had been for her.

Chapter Twelve

Somehow, Hannah managed to fall asleep that night, in spite of the tossing and turning, the images of Belterre's unhappy face and the kernels of questions that kept bursting like popcorn in her head. But it was only to dream of ringing telephones that she could never answer in time and kitchen sinks brimming with salty tears.

Next morning at breakfast, Belterre greeted Hannah with her usual cheerful smile as she placed a bowl of porridge on the table. But her eyes betrayed her once again. They were clouded with an emotion that Hannah couldn't quite identify.

"Porridge again?" asked Hannah, as Bel set the bowl down.

"Of course, dear. My children have always

started their day with a bowl of porridge and you're just like one of my own. So eat up and don't complain!" She tugged on a strand of Hannah's hair.

"I'm not complaining," said Hannah, reaching for a spoon. "As long as there's plenty of brown sugar and cream around."

"Well I'm complaining!" Jake was standing in the doorway, rubbing his eyes. "I'm tired of porridge, Bel. All I want is a bowl of cereal or something. Don't you have anything sweet?"

"All I've got is bran flakes and puffed wheat," Bel told him. "So eat your porridge and quit complaining."

Jake slumped into a chair and started dumping sugar and cream into his bowl of porridge. Then he started to complain again.

"We haven't even *been* to the beach yet and it's almost time to go home. Everyone's too busy and we're running out of time. Now there's only today and tomorrow left. When *are* we going to the beach, Bel. Remember? You always make a great picnic lunch and we go down there and swim and build sandcastles. Well, you never come, but Willie always does."

"You know it's too cool to swim," Bel reminded him. "But, if your parents agree, then I'm sure you'll be able to have a Christmas beach picnic before you go back. Maybe this afternoon. I've got some chicken left over from last night's supper. And some fresh buns, too."

"Yay," whooped Jake. He scooped a spoonful of porridge into his mouth and made a face. "Why *don't* you ever come to the beach, Bel? Don't you like it? I don't think you've *ever* been with us."

"You know I find it too hot and windy for my liking," Belterre said with a shrug. "I'd rather stay up here where it's nice and cool."

"It's not very hot at this time of year," said Hannah. "I was down there the other day with Maya and Cassie. It was nice and cool, Bel. Just the right temperature for you. I think you should come this time."

Suddenly, Belterre became very busy wiping down the benchtop.

"Bel? How about it?" Hannah tapped on her bowl to get Belterre's attention. "Yoo hoo! Hello in there! Will you come with us? It'll be like a little Christmas celebration." Silence. "Did you hear me, Belterre?"

"I heard you just fine," Belterre said to the benchtop. "And I'll think about it, okay, Hannah? Just don't ask me for an answer right now."

Hannah and Jake looked at each other and Jake shrugged and pushed his bowl of porridge away. As Hannah scooped the last of the porridge into her mouth, she watched Bel wipe the spotless benchtop over and over again, with slow, even strokes.

"Well? What did he say?"

Hannah had barely unlatched the garden gate for Maya later that morning when the question came tumbling out. Maya didn't bother with a polite hello first.

"And a good morning to you, too, Papaya," replied Hannah. "What did *who* say, anyway? What are we talking about?"

"We're talking about Ernie Johnson. The guy who phoned you last night, dodo. What did he have to say about Belterre and Martha Cox? What did he tell you?"

"I think those little knots of hair on your head are too tight. I don't know anyone named Ernie

… whoever. And nobody phoned me … um …I don't think."

The two girls flopped down on the cedar bench. Hannah stared out at the shimmering sea.

"Um … "

"Um?" repeated Maya. "That's your answer?"

"No," said Hannah. "My answer is *yes*. Someone did ring the house last night, but I didn't answer it. Belterre did. And she told the caller, whoever it was, that there was nobody here by the name they wanted. In fact, she told us that the caller was Santa Claus! Could that have been this Ernie, Maya?"

Maya nibbled her lip. "It could have been, I guess. But why wouldn't my grandmother give you the phone?"

"That's what I'm trying to figure out. Maybe she didn't hear right. Maybe he mispronounced my name."

"Who could mispronounce the name Hannah Hawthorne? He repeated it twice when I told him." Maya shook her head. "Maybe it wasn't him after all."

"She was looking right at me when she

answered the phone, Maya. She looked sort of guilty, then she turned away and spoke in a lower voice. Wait a minute!" Hannah pinched Maya's arm. "Who is this guy anyway?"

"Ouch! You've got my attention! Trust me, you don't have to pinch me!" Maya rubbed the sore spot on her skin. "He's the lighthouse keeper's son," she said. "Or at least he was. A long time ago, when there *was* a lighthouse keeper."

"The lighthouse keeper's son? Why would he be ringing me? What does he have to do with Martha Cox and the rest of the crazy story? Is he a ghost, too?"

Maya rolled her eyes. "This guy, Ernie Johnson, used to be a friend of Belterre's. A long time ago. But he hasn't seen her or spoken to her in decades. He owns a little gift shop not far from here. I spoke to him after I got home yesterday."

"But how did you know about him, if Bel hasn't seen him in so long?"

"Because of her stories," explained Maya. "She always used to tell me stories about what it was like to grow up on the island a long time ago. How they used to go barefoot everywhere, even to school. And how they learned their times tables by singing them. And the silly names of the silly games they used to play. Like Piggy in the Middle and Sally in the Barn. And how one of her best friends was this lighthouse keeper's son named Ernie Johnson. She used to tell me about all the fun things that they used to do."

"Right." Hannah nodded. "Bel used to tell me all kinds of stories, too, when we came for our summer holiday. But I liked the ones about ghosts the best, so I made her tell them over and over again. I think I remember something about a lighthouse keeper's son, though, but she never mentioned his name."

"Well, she did mention it to me, so I looked in the phone book and I actually found the guy! After a couple of wrong numbers, of course."

"You're kidding me!" said Hannah. "So what did you find out?"

"Well, nothing, actually," admitted Maya. "There were customers in his gift shop and he couldn't stay on the phone. But he said he knew Bel very well once upon a time. I told him that we might like to ask him some questions and he agreed. So I gave him your number so you could set up a time, since you only have a couple of days left here before you go home."

"Good plan," Hannah said. "Except that I never got to talk to him. So now what? Maybe he thinks you were just messing around on the phone, crank calling him or something."

Maya winked at Hannah and dug into the pocket of her shorts. She pulled out a tiny piece of paper that was folded many times. "Ta da!" she said. "I saved his phone number. Maybe you should phone him?"

"As soon as I can get near the phone without Belterre listening over my shoulder. It's a pity the phone's in the kitchen because she's always there." Hannah paused and gazed out again at the azure water and the distant waves ruffling the shore. "It's still bugging me, you know, Maya," she said after a moment. "That Bel didn't let me take that call. I just don't get it!"

"Well, maybe you will, after you talk to Ernie. Maybe he'll be able to clear some things up."

"Hope so." Hannah sighed. "Because never, in all the years that I've known her, have I seen Belterre acting so strangely. And it's only since the name Martha Cox came up a few days ago. So I'm not resting until I find out why."

Maya tapped her fingers on the arm of the bench. "I think I've got a better idea than a phone call. How about a picnic lunch at the lighthouse? That could be our excuse, anyway. And, after our picnic, we'll just take a little scooter ride along the coast to Ernie Johnson's gift shop."

"Right. And we can ring him first, just to let him know that we're coming. Now that," said Hannah, rubbing her hands together, "sounds like a plan!"

Chapter Thirteen

"Why can't we go? We always go to the beach when we're in Bermuda. It's not fair!" Hannah and Maya were greeted by Jake's whining voice when they went inside to make some sandwiches for lunch. Bel was already slicing bread at the bench and setting out plates of cold chicken for everyone else.

"You don't seem to understand." Their mother was speaking in a calm, even voice. "There is nobody who can take you this time, Jake. Willie has to take Belterre shopping and your dad and I have to meet with the estate agent this afternoon."

"That stinks," said Jake. He cast a mournful glance at Hannah and Maya.

"Don't look at us," said Hannah. "We're going for a picnic to the lighthouse. We just came inside to pack our lunches."

"Can I come, too?" he begged.

"Sorry, bud," said Maya, ruffling his hair. "No room on the scooter. But I promise I'll take you for a ride when we get back."

"That stinks, too. That means I'm stuck here alone."

Dad slapped his hand on the kitchen table and everyone jumped. "There's no need to be rude, Jake," he said. "You're not winning anyone's sympathy with that attitude."

Jake's lip curled into a sulky snarl. "I could go alone, you know. I'm twelve years old. That's old enough to go to the beach alone. I know my way. And if it's too cold to swim, I'll just go and sit on the rocks. And I'm a really good swimmer anyway, so even if … "

The knife clattered from Belterre's hand to the floor and she turned to face Jake. "You must never, *ever*, go to the beach by yourself. How many times have I told you that? It's absolutely forbidden. It is *not* a place for little children." She cupped Jake's chin gently in her hand.

"But I'm not a little child," whispered Jake.

"Did you hear me, son?" Bel stared deep into his eyes.

Jake gazed back at her, unblinking. "I heard you, Bel."

"Good," said Belterre. Then she picked up her knife, rinsed it and continued slicing without another word.

Everyone was silent for a moment, and then Willie cleared his throat. "You can come with me when I take Bel shopping, Jake," he said, grinning broadly. "I could sure use the company."

"Thanks, but no thanks," said Jake. "I've shopped enough this week. I'll stay here and read about ghosts."

"Look, Jake," said Dad in a soothing voice, "I know how much you like the beach and we'll do our best to get there. But you know how busy we've been. I didn't even get to play golf!" He shook his head in disbelief. "We shouldn't be too late at our meeting this afternoon, so maybe there'll still be time when we get back. And there's always tomorrow if we're not too busy. So get a grip, kiddo."

"I won't hold my breath," Hannah heard Jake mutter as he spun on his heel and stomped out of the room.

"Well. That was quite pleasant, wasn't it?"

said Hannah, trying to make everyone laugh.

It didn't work. But, when everyone followed Jake out of the room to try to calm him down, Maya dug the piece of paper out of her pocket and made a quick phone call to Ernie Johnson. As she hung up, she shot Hannah a "thumbs up".

"It's all set, Banana," she said. "Let's hit the road."

It was a perfect day for a picnic. Hannah and Maya tucked their lunch into the storage compartment under the scooter's seat.

"Make sure you've got those helmets fastened securely," Willie called to them from the front door as they were leaving.

"Don't worry, Grandpa," Maya called back.

"Your granddaughter's a safe driver, Willie," Hannah added, as she climbed on to the seat behind Maya and her friend started the motor.

She waved as they rolled out on to the Tribe Road and set off for the lighthouse. Once again, a little flurry of excitement danced in Hannah's stomach at the feeling of independence these rides gave her. It was another one of the good things about Bermuda, the scooter rides and the fun she had with Maya, and Hannah made a mental note to add it to her good points list. *Along with meeting ghosts and beach picnics. And tea at the lighthouse and Bel's awesome chowder.* Now, it seemed, the list of good points was getting longer than the list of bad ones.

Just as they turned on to South Road, they passed Cassie wheeling her bike towards Belterre's place. Maya stopped her scooter by the roadside and cut the motor.

"Hi, Cassie! Where are you going?"

"I was coming to see you, Maya," replied Cassie. "Your mother told me you were here, but it looks like you two are headed out." Hannah was sure she detected a frown when Cassie looked at her. "Where are you going?"

"For a picnic at the lighthouse," said Maya.

"Hmm. Guess I'll go over and visit Jake then. And listen to more of his ghost stories. He told me all about this Martha Cox lady, the ghost you *thought* you saw the other day, Hannah." Cassie rolled her eyes.

I did see her, Hannah wanted to say, but the

thought of further teasing from Cassie put her off and she bit her tongue instead.

"Actually, visiting Jake is a great idea. He's having a hissy fit because he can't go for a beach picnic today and he's stuck home alone. Maybe you'll be able to drag him out of his rotten mood," suggested Maya.

"I'll do my best," said Cassie and pedalled away.

"That should keep him happy for a while," said Hannah. "At least now he'll have somebody to complain to instead of just the walls!"

It was around one-thirty that afternoon when the fragrances started to bother Hannah.

The girls had slowly started to pack up the remains of their feast by the lighthouse, though Maya was still chewing on a piece of loquat cake. As they both gazed out across the sparkling bay, Hannah began to sniff the air.

"Are you wearing perfume?" she asked, leaning over to sniff Maya's neck.

"Get out of it," said Maya, nudging her away with a sharp elbow. "I never wear perfume, even though we have a perfumery right here on the island. I'd rather smell the flowers instead of smelling *like* one! Besides," she said, sniffing the air, "I don't smell anything right now."

"Well, someone's wearing perfume," insisted Hannah. She glanced quickly over her shoulder as if the culprit might be standing right behind her. "That's ... very weird ... " she murmured slowly. "It's just like ... like whatever I smelled ... the day I saw Martha Cox. I'm sure it is. I'd recognise it anywhere."

"It is?" whispered Maya. "You're sure?"

"I'll never forget it," Hannah told her. Goose bumps bloomed on her arms and she shivered. "Let's head over to see Ernie Johnson before I chicken out and change my mind."

Hannah gave the air one more tentative sniff then blew her nose into a paper napkin, trying her best to chase away the strangely familiar aroma. She helped Maya finish packing up and in a few minutes they were whizzing along the South Road once again in the direction of Ernie's shop.

The smell was still there. It stayed with her all through the ride, even as the wind rushed over her face. It became so strong, Hannah didn't even pay any attention to the spectacular view of pink beaches and aqua surf along the South Shore.

Something was tickling her thoughts, too, making it hard to concentrate. It was a nagging feeling of something left undone — an uneasy feeling, like when she hadn't studied enough before a test. And, no matter how hard she tried to shake the feeling, it kept welling up inside her, pushing out everything else from her mind.

This is crazy, thought Hannah. *I've got ghosts on the brain. I swear, even my head is being haunted by Martha Cox!*

Ernie Johnson's gift shop was tucked into a hillside near the road, overlooking a gleaming stretch of beach. Maya pulled up beside three other scooters parked in front and switched off the engine.

"This is it," she said, unstrapping her helmet. "I hope you know what you're going to say to him, Hannah."

"Me? I can't even think straight right now. Who knows what kind of jumbled up gibberish is going to pour out of my mouth. Can't *you* ask him about Martha?" begged Hannah.

"Hey, kid." Maya patted Hannah's shoulder. "This is *your* story and it's up to *you* to find out how it ends. I just came along for the ride."

Hannah took a deep breath. Then, staring straight ahead, she marched quickly towards the gift shop door, pulled it open and stepped into the cool room.

Her eyes took a moment to adjust to the sudden dimness as Maya edged in behind her. Across the room, a few tourists were paying for their purchases at the counter. The tall man behind the till was chatting with them as he punched in prices. The shop was a jumbled assortment of collectables and curiosities. There were the usual T-shirts, postcards, mugs and saltwater toffee, as well as shell, fish and dolphin-shaped jewellery, pottery and small souvenirs made from Bermuda cedar.

Hannah leaned over the jewellery display, and pretended to be shopping as she tried to catch a better glimpse of the man she supposed was Ernie Johnson. She spotted a silver bracelet in the form of a circle of leaping dolphins all joined together.

"Look," she said, pointing it out to Maya. "I love this bracelet. You know how much I love dolphins. I should have brought my wallet!"

"Never mind that right now," Maya whispered near Hannah's ear. "We've got bigger fish to fry." She snickered at her own joke and Hannah was just about to remind her that a dolphin was actually a mammal when a deep voice boomed across the shop.

"Maya, Maya, Maya! I've been expecting you!"

"How did he know it was me?" whispered Maya to Hannah. "He's never seen me before."

Hannah shrugged. "Beats me!"

"I'd know you anywhere, Maya," he boomed as he walked towards them. "You look just like your grandma Bel did so many years ago. I'm Ernie."

He towered over them. His face was as brown and shiny as a chestnut, and creased with a wide bright smile. As he introduced himself, he held out a hand that was as broad as a dinner plate.

"So happy to meet you, Maya," he said and nearly shook her arm off. "So happy to meet one of Belterre's relatives, at long last." Then he wrapped his lanky arms around her and hugged her hard. "It seems I've been waiting forever."

"Pleased to meet you, sir," said Maya, gazing up at him, wide-eyed.

"Sir! I'm not a sir! I'm just Ernie. Just plain old Ernie."

"Well … uh … Ernie," said Maya, with a grin. "I'd like you to meet my friend, Hannah Banana!"

"Hannah Banana. How do you do?" Hannah's hand disappeared into Ernie's like a baseball in a catcher's mitt and he bowed. "So sorry we couldn't speak the other night."

"Me, too," said Hannah. "I was standing right there, you know. I don't know what was the matter with Belterre, pretending it was a wrong number."

"Well, maybe we can get to the bottom of it today," said Ernie. "Let's find ourselves a seat. I've got some pretty interesting stories to share."

Chapter Fourteen

Ernie led them out to the back of the shop where a weathered table and chairs of Bermuda cedar were grouped against a backdrop of vivid pink oleander and bougainvillea bushes. The table was already set with a jug of orange juice and three glasses as well as a plate heaped with oatmeal cookies.

"Sit down, please. Make yourselves at home," he said.

"But who'll mind your shop?" asked Hannah, as she settled herself on a chair.

"Oh, Betty's in there," said Ernie. "My wife. We live upstairs, you know. She'll take care of things while you're here Then I'll take you back inside to meet her." Ernie poured them each a glass of juice, then passed around the cookies. "Now," he said, rubbing his hands together.

"I'm ready if you are, Hannah. Tell me what's on your mind and I'll help you if I can."

All the confusing thoughts that had been swirling around in Hannah's head since her first encounter with Martha Cox came streaming out as soon as she opened her mouth. She told him about that first tumble in the bushes, about Martha's kind eyes and the smell of flowers, about Jake's spill on the road and the strange pushing sensation from behind. She explained about their trip to the library and how they had learned more details about Martha's tragic life.

Ernie listened quietly, his kind face rumpled with concern. He seemed to know not to interrupt her rambling tale with questions. When she reached the part about Belterre and her tear-filled eyes, her reluctance to talk about Martha, he nodded slowly, but didn't say a word.

"And then you rang," said Hannah. "And I had the feeling the phone call was for me, because of the strange way she looked at me. But she didn't give me a chance to speak to you."

Ernie was still nodding. "That's right," he said. "Because she did know it was me. I told her my name. And she didn't want me to speak to you, Hannah. So she let on that I had the wrong number. I even said her name and asked how she was, but she said she couldn't hear me very well."

"But why, Ernie?" Maya was frowning. "Why would she do that? That's not like my grandmother at all."

"She's one of the warmest people I've ever met," added Hannah.

Ernie tapped a long finger on the table. "Maybe so. But something's eating her up inside. Has been for years. That's why she hasn't spoken to me for more than half a century. And that's a long time, a very long time, to be carrying something around like that."

"Carrying what around?" Hannah touched his hand. "Tell us, Ernie."

Ernie sighed and scratched his head. "Belterre and I were the best of friends. The very best of friends, long long ago. I lived at the lighthouse and my father was the keeper there. A whole group of us used to play together, but Bel, who was the only girl among us, was always the ring leader. She was the one with all the bright ideas. She decided what games we'd play. She always packed our lunches when she led us off on little expeditions. If we hurt ourselves, she would be the nurse. If someone had a problem, she would offer advice. And she always told us stories, too. She was a wonderful companion."

"She's still the same way," said Maya. "Likes to be in charge. Loves to tell stories and give advice. And makes great lunches!"

"I can just imagine." Ernie tried to grin, but his eyes were dark with sadness.

As Hannah watched and listened, she tried her best to ignore the fragrance in the air that seemed to be growing stronger. *Just the flowers in the hedge,* she kept telling herself. *It's just those beautiful flowers that I'm smelling.* And she might have convinced herself if it weren't for the restless, trembling feeling in her arms and legs, as if she had a severe case of the jitters.

Be quiet, crazy brain, she told herself. *Leave me alone and listen to Ernie's story.* What was he saying now? Something about a terrible day?

"What was that?" interrupted Hannah, trying to shake the muzziness from her head. "Sorry, I missed it. What did you just say, Ernie?"

"I said that everything changed on that

terrible day," Ernie replied.

Maya leaned forward. "What day?"

"On that day … that day that the Cox boys drowned," whispered Ernie. He stared at the table, wouldn't look at them.

"You mean … " Hannah was afraid to say it. "You mean the two of you were there that day? You and Belterre?"

"That's right. Bel and I were there when it happened."

Somewhere nearby a kiskadee was calling. A gentle December wind shivered through the bushes and wisps of cirrus clouds drifted across the sky above them. No one spoke. They all stared at the rough grey surface of the table. Hannah felt as though someone had clamped a strong hand around her throat.

Suddenly, everything was starting to make sense – the tears in Bel's eyes, her reluctance to talk about Martha, the way she always avoided going to the beach.

"You were both there that day," murmured Hannah. "But it was her idea, wasn't it? It was one of her little expeditions. She probably even packed the lunch for everyone, didn't she, Ernie?"

"That's right, Hannah." Ernie's voice was hoarse now, and Hannah didn't dare to look at him. "It was Bel's idea, because she was always in charge, you see. She decided when we'd go and when we'd leave. And we always listened to her. It was a beautiful day and we were climbing around on the rocks, just like we always did. The tide was starting to come in, but we were having so much fun, we didn't pay attention. When we finally noticed, the cove had filled up.

"Bel and Sammie and I made it back to the beach, but Robbie was afraid and stayed behind. The water was getting deeper, covering up the rock. So Sammie tried to swim back and help his brother. They never made it. And there was nothing we could do to help them."

"It wasn't her fault though, Ernie." Maya's cheeks were wet with tears. "It's easy to get carried away when you're having fun. I do it all the time."

"We all do, dear," agreed Ernie, patting her hand. "We all do now and then."

Hannah's heart was trying to thump its way out of her chest. She clenched her fists. "Something's wrong," she said. They both looked over at her.

"Something's wrong, right now. I can feel it. I can smell it. I know it."

"What are you talking about?" Maya was staring at her. "Is it the flowers? You still smell flowers?"

Hannah nodded. "And there's other stuff, too. Sorry to cut our visit short, Ernie, but I think we should go. I just feel like we should be home." She stood up, stamped her feet, shook her arms out. "I think we should hurry, Maya," she said.

The scooter ride home was just a blur to Hannah. She clung to the seat and stared at Maya's back instead of the passing scenery, the nagging uneasiness fluttering in her chest. An urgent voice in her head was repeating the word *hurry* over and over again. The overpowering scent of flowers made her feel as though she'd inhaled a bottle of perfume. Now they were zipping past the dangerous curve in the road where Hannah had tumbled off her bike a few days ago. And saw Martha Cox.

Some say that Martha Cox warns people. That she

tries to stop the same thing from happening to them. What did Belterre mean when she said "the same thing"? It could mean anything, Hannah tried to reassure herself. *It doesn't have anything to do with the horrible story that Ernie just told us. Martha's warning doesn't have anything to do with her little boys who died at the beach half a century ago.*

It felt as though a thick band was tightening around Hannah's throat as she tried to dismiss the thoughts invading her head like so many weeds, smothering everything that seemed rational and sane. *He wouldn't go to the beach alone. Jake just isn't dumb enough to do that. Is he? Is he? Is he? Is he?*

"Cassie's with him," Hannah murmured into the rushing wind. "So what am I worrying about? She's from the island. She knows what she's doing. She'll keep an eye on him."

When they reached Willie and Bel's house, Hannah hopped off the scooter and bolted before Maya even stopped the motor. Willie's taxi was nowhere in sight. The front door was flung open. Parcels were strewn on the porch, dropped there, not even carried inside.

Hannah picked them up as she stepped into

the shadowy coolness of the hallway. Now she could see Belterre, standing in the kitchen. One hand rested on her throat, the other clutched a crumpled piece of paper. Her eyes stared unseeing, glazed with something like dread.

"He's gone." Belterre's voice was a hoarse whisper.

"Who's gone? Where?" Maya's voice came from behind Hannah. "What's going on, Grandma?"

"He's gone? By himself?" Hannah set down the parcels and reached for the piece of paper that Belterre held out to her.

The note was scrawled in Jake's sloppy hand-writing. *Going to the beach with Cassie. I'm riding Bel's crazy old bike! We packed some cake and drinks. Be back soon, so don't worry. Jake.*

"It was taped to the front door. Oh, why did he go there alone after I warned him?" moaned Belterre.

"Bel. Don't worry." Hannah tried to reassure her, in spite of her own creeping fear. "He's with Cassie and she knows what she's doing. They'll be fine."

"Um. Not exactly," said Maya softly.

"Not exactly what?" There was a hard edge to Hannah's voice now that she couldn't control. She scrunched Jake's note up in a tight, damp fist. "Not exactly what, Maya?"

"Uh ... she ... might not exactly know what she's doing."

"Why not?"

"Because ... she's not exactly *from* Bermuda. She's from Canada. Like you. She started school here in September. Her family's staying for two years, just like your family." Maya couldn't look at Hannah and stared at the floor instead.

"But why was it such a big secret? What was the big deal, Maya?"

"We were going to tell you tomorrow. On your last day. We wanted to show you how easy it is to fit in here. We let you believe that Cassie's been living here all her life to show you how easy it is to adapt to the island. I'm sorry, Hannah. It was just a stupid joke."

"Forget it," said Hannah, turning away from her. "It's not important right now. Where's Willie, Bel?"

Belterre had sunk into a chair. "He dropped me off without coming inside. He had to go back to work, so he doesn't know." She paused, sniffed the air. "Can … can you smell them, girls? Can you smell the … the flowers right now? I haven't smelled them in years."

Hannah touched Bel's shoulder. "I smell them. I've been smelling them all afternoon. What does it mean, Bel?" She knew, but she didn't want to believe it, wanted to hear it from someone else.

"It means that she's nearby. She's trying to warn us that something's wrong."

Hannah's limbs felt odd, as limp as over-cooked noodles. It was an effort to force her legs to walk in the direction of the front door. She caught hold of Maya's hand and squeezed it hard.

"Let's go, Maya. And let's hurry. You wait here, Bel. And please don't worry yourself. Everything will be fine."

Clinging to Maya's hand as they hustled through the doorway, Hannah desperately wished she could believe her own words.

Chapter Fifteen

The car park at the beach was deserted. Hannah started to run as soon as her feet hit the pavement and Maya wasn't far behind. In a moment, they were standing in the sunshine beside two abandoned bicycles that had been dropped at the end of the beach path. The girls scanned a stretch of empty sand and distant rocks.

"Their bikes are here. But where *are* they, Maya?" Hannah dug her fingers into Maya's arm.

"Don't panic." Maya wrapped her arm around Hannah's waist. "We haven't reached the rocks yet. Cassie and Jake are probably just playing in the cove and haven't noticed how late it's getting."

They kicked off their shoes and dashed barefoot across the warm sand. When they reached the rock tunnel that led to the cove, they waded knee-deep into the water. Showered by icy spray from the crashing surf, Hannah and Maya gazed out over the rocks that jutted up from the sea like the craggy heads of giants.

As she squinted into the sunshine, Hannah felt a growing sense of dread churning in her stomach. The cove had filled with swirling water. Most of the rocks were already covered. The easy escape route over the lowest boulders was all but swallowed by the sea and only the highest rocks were left protruding, surrounded by dangerous cracks and crevasses too wide to jump over safely.

And there, waving frantically from the top of the rocks, were Jake and Cassie.

"Oh no." Hannah groped for Maya's hand. "They're stuck there. And the water's almost reached them. We need to get help!"

"We can't both go." Maya shook her hand free from Hannah's. "One of us has to stay here and keep them in sight. In case the water reaches them and they have to swim."

"It's just like what happened to Ernie and Belterre," whispered Hannah. Her body felt weak and wobbly, as if all her energy had leaked away. *They never made it. And there was nothing we could do to help them.* Ernie's solemn words echoed in her head. *Never made it. Never made it.*

All around her, the fragrance of flowers swirled in the ocean breeze. A voice murmured past her ears, tangled up with the wind and the rhythmic splashing of the waves. An indistinct voice that whispered urgently, *Hurry. Hurry. Hurry, Hannah, hurry.* A shiver of fear danced down her arms.

"You go," she told Maya. "You've got the scooter. And hurry."

"But what about you?"

"I'll stay here and watch them," said Hannah. "I'll figure something out."

Maya grabbed both of Hannah's hands and shook her arms, trying to wrench her gaze from the direction of the rocks. She stared into her eyes.

"Look at me. Now promise you won't do anything stupid, Hannah." Hannah's eyes veered back to the jagged rocks and rising water that held Cassie and her brother hostage. Maya shook Hannah's arms again. "Promise me? Okay? I won't be long."

"Okay," Hannah muttered in the direction of the cove.

Maya ran, her long legs striding, feet churning up the sand. Hannah watched only until she reached the path to the car park. Then she turned her eyes back to Jake and Cassie.

"There must be something I can do to help them," she said.

Hannah scrambled up the closest rock, slipping as she struggled for a foothold and skinning her knees on the rough surface. She yelled in their direction.

"Stay put, Jake! Maya's gone for help!" The words blew back in her face, never came close to reaching the prisoners stranded on the rocks. Now Jake had caught sight of her and stood up.

"Sit down," screamed Hannah. "You'll slip!"

Jake couldn't hear her. He cupped his hands to his ears and made a shrugging gesture. Then, to Hannah's disbelief, he flailed his arms in a swimming motion, before swinging them forward as if he were about to jump.

Cassie stood up, too, and they seemed to argue for a moment. Cassie was tugging on his T-shirt, trying to prevent him from leaping into the cove, but, just as he had on the road when he'd nearly been hit by Willie, Jake wrestled himself out of her grasp.

"Don't do it, Jake," shouted Hannah. "This time, *don't do it!*" But her words went sweeping away like smoke on the wind.

And then Jake did it. He jumped.

Hannah sucked in a gulp of air as she watched him disappear feet first into the water. In a moment, his head was bobbing above the surface, and she let her breath seep out once more. *He's a good swimmer,* she reminded herself. *He's a strong swimmer. He's been taking lessons for years, just like me. And water safety, too.*

Water safety. Never swim alone. Use the buddy system. Life-saving techniques. One by one, the words exploded like firecrackers in her head until she found the one she needed. *Lifebuoy. Lifebuoy. Every beach has lifebuoys.*

And this one had them, too. Hanging on red posts along the beach. You weren't supposed to touch them unless someone got into trouble.

"And someone is in trouble right now," muttered Hannah, as she slithered down the rock and began to dash along the beach in the hard wet sand. "If he has to swim this far, he'll probably need it."

She grabbed two of them. They were larger and heavier than she expected, but, with a sudden spurt of energy bolstered by the urgent messages in her head, she wrapped them in her arms and raced back across the sand to the rocky outcrop.

Jake was halfway across the cove now, propelling himself through the waves with the strong crawl stroke he always used in freestyle swimming races. In the distance, Cassie was crouched, a lonely figure abandoned on the slowly vanishing rock.

As Jake neared the shore, he slowed and began spluttering and waving. Hannah tossed the life-buoy as hard as she could and watched it fall hopelessly short. The tide was soon nudging it back towards the beach.

And then suddenly, Jake was standing waist-deep in the breaking waves, doubled over and gasping for breath. Hannah waded in to meet him, oblivious to the chilly water lapping at the cuffs of her shorts. She grabbed hold of his arm and yanked him to shore, not sure if she wanted to hug him or to yell at him. She decided to do both.

"Jake, you fool! Why did you swim to shore? Are you nuts? Can't you remember what Bel always tells us? You should have waited on the rock!" Hannah wrapped her arms around him and he sniffled into her neck, returning the hug. He was shivering, and when she stepped back to look at him his lips were blue.

"C-C-C-C …" he stammered through his shivers. "It's C-C-Cassie. She c-c-can't swim. You h-h-have to h-h-help her!"

"Can't swim? Then she'll just have to wait on the rock until Maya gets here with help," said Hannah. Jake pointed in the direction of the rock and Hannah spun around. "Oh, no," she murmured.

The tide had crept up higher than ever. Now Cassie was standing and the waves were licking at her feet. She was waving both arms frantically, screaming towards them. Hannah was sure she heard the words *help me* being tossed across the water by the brisk sea wind.

Hannah went down the beach to retrieve the lifebuoy and dumped it beside the hunched, shivering Jake. "What should I do?" she asked. "The lifebuoy couldn't possibly reach that far if

I try to throw it."

"I'll s-s-swim b-b-back," stuttered Jake. "I'll t-t-take her a l-l-lifebuoy!" His whole body was vibrating as he stumbled back into the water.

Never made it. Never made it. The words echoed in Hannah's mind once more as the fragrances swirled around her and her body buzzed with an unfamiliar energy. She shook her arms and stamped her feet, as if she could shake the feeling off like the sand sticking to her damp skin. *Hurry, Hannah, hurry. Before it's too late.* The words sighed in her ears like a message whispered from the past. *Some say she warns people, warns people, warns people.*

"No," said Hannah. She grabbed Jake's arm. "You can't. You're frozen and you're scared. I'm afraid you might go into shock. You have to sit here in the sun and wait for Maya. And keep an eye on me, because I'm going out there to get her. Okay?"

"B-b-but … "

"No b-b-buts, Jake," said Hannah firmly. Don't budge till I get back." She eased him gently back on to the warm sand. "Stay out of the wind. It's sheltered by the rocks here. I know it's almost impossible for you to sit still, but this time you're going to have to listen to me. So don't move!"

"Ok-k-kay," agreed Jake reluctantly.

Hannah made a quick reef knot with the rope from one of the lifebuoys, tying it securely around her waist. Then she flung the other one into the water ahead of her and plunged into the foamy surf, gasping at the sudden chill.

I can't let this happen again, she told herself as she clung to the lifebuoy and frog-kicked towards the distant rock. *It would destroy Bel if the same thing happened here again. I've got to reach Cassie before the tide does.*

Salt water stung her eyes and streamed down her face, half-blinding her. Every so often, a swell would churn over her head and engulf her. Still she focused on the distant rock, trying her best to keep Cassie in view.

"Halfway there," she told herself. "Halfway there." A huge wave rolled over her head and the sky, the rock and all sense of direction vanished for an instant as she kicked and bobbed in the restless sea. By the time she had the last remaining patch of the rock in sight, Cassie was gone.

Where is she? Where is she? The words screamed in her head before she could scream them into the wind. "Cassie! Where are you?" And once more her cries blew back in her face, along with a choking mouthful of salty water. Hannah gurgled and spluttered, coughing out the sea water as she tried to catch her breath, kicking hard, trying not to lose her momentum as her eyes scanned the water for Cassie. And then at last she spotted a bobbing head, a stretching arm, sinking, rising up again, signalling a desperate plea for help. Was she too far away to make it in time? Could she get close enough to grab hold and pluck her from the swirling tide? *Never made it. Never made it. A very long time to be carrying around something like that.*

Hannah closed her eyes and kicked. A vision of sad, dark eyes floated in the grey wavering light behind her eyelids. They were Martha Cox's eyes, gentle and concerned, silently transmitting her urgent message. *Some say she warns people. Tries to stop the same thing from happening to them.* And now they were Belterre's eyes, frightened, mournful, shining with tears. *You must never, ever go to the beach by yourself. Absolutely forbidden.*

Was this what it had all been leading up to? Was it?

A determined burst of power sent her surging forward. Strong thrusts from her legs propelled her towards Cassie's floundering form until she seemed to be close enough. Hannah reeled in the lifebuoy she had been towing, heaved it over her head and pitched it across the water. It spun towards Cassie, spraying a shimmer of droplets, then skipped like a stone to land barely a metre away from her.

"Grab it, Cassie!" screamed Hannah. The top of Cassie's head was still visible, her nose just clearing the surface of the water. A pair of terrified eyes locked on to Hannah's. Then a weary arm groped for and closed over the ring. And every last ounce of energy drained out of Hannah like the air seeping out of a balloon.

Chapter Sixteen

Hannah wasn't sure how long she floated like a piece of driftwood in the cove, clinging to the lifebuoy. Aware that Cassie was safely hanging on to one of the rings herself, wafting up and down in the swells beside her, Hannah was finally able to relax. She closed her eyes and drifted there, not even feeling the chill, as the restlessness and dread that had been haunting her all day slowly ebbed away and a welcome peace calmed her busy brain.

And the smell was gone. The mystifying scent of Martha Cox had vanished as soon as Cassie wrapped her arm around the lifebuoy. Hannah missed it already, and the reassuring sense of Martha's presence.

But I suppose I don't need her now, thought Hannah. *She's done her job. This time we both made it.*

When she opened her eyes, she was facing the shore. There was a group of people standing there, some jumping up and down and waving, desperately trying to attract her attention. They seemed to be yelling, but she couldn't hear the words, so she waved at them and a shriek of joy echoed, loud and clear, across the water.

"Cassie?" called Hannah. "Do you think you can paddle back now or should I tow you?"

"It's okay," said Cassie, her faint voice barely carrying on the wind. "I can paddle beside you. I'll be fine."

"Well let's go," said Hannah, "because there seems to be a whole welcoming party waiting to greet us on the shore!"

Tired from her ordeal, Cassie churned slowly through the water in silence until at last the beach grew near. Then she looked over at Hannah and inhaled deeply. "You saved me," she said. "Thanks so much, Hannah."

Hannah didn't answer. She just smiled at Cassie and nodded, trying her best to forget the silly joke that she and Maya had been teasing her with for the past few days.

The beach was crowded with people, and

Hannah tried to identify the faces.

"My parents are there," said Cassie, just as some of the waiting crowd came wading out into the surf to meet them with armfuls of towels.

Maya was there, too, and her parents and Hannah's. Hannah's mum had her arms wrapped tightly around Jake, who was now swaddled in a huge, fluffy towel. Willie stood beside them, his face still creased with lines of worry.

"And is that Belterre?" murmured Hannah to herself, wonderingly. "With Ernie Johnson? It can't be! Bel never comes to the beach!"

But it *was* Bel. And, as soon as Hannah waded into the shallows, she rushed out to meet her, splashing through the water in her sandals, wrapping her arms around Hannah and sobbing into her neck.

"Oh, child. I knew that something was going to happen. I knew, from the flowers and the fidgety feeling I got as soon as you started to talk about Martha Cox. I should have told you! I should have told you the whole story! Then maybe we could have stopped this from happening again. I'm so sorry. So very, very sorry."

"It's okay, Bel," said Hannah, returning the embrace as she led her back to the beach. "It's over now and nothing bad has happened. Everything turned out fine this time."

"I warned you not to do anything stupid, Hannah!" exclaimed Maya, as she hugged her friend. "But I'm glad you took the chance!"

"I told you when I got to your house, Bel." Ernie placed a heavy hand on Hannah and Maya's shoulder. "I told you that these two girls have sensible heads. That you didn't have to worry. That history wouldn't repeat itself."

"I know," said Bel, sinking slowly on to the warm sand. "But I just couldn't bring myself to believe it. And that's why I made you bring me here, Ernie. I had to see for myself."

Everyone who had rushed to the beach sat down in the sand and formed a protective circle around Hannah and Belterre. Hannah felt someone drape a towel over her shoulders, but she was too intent on comforting Bel to notice who it was. Bel hunched cross-legged, her dress billowing over her knees, and Hannah watched as a single tear trickled down her shiny cheek and splashed on to the sand. She caught hold of Bel's big, callused hands and squeezed them gently.

"Bel," she said. "Everyone is all right. We're all here. You don't have to worry any more."

"I'm not worried," murmured Bel. "I'm just sad and sorry. Sad about all the grief I've caused over the years. Sorry that I've neglected poor Ernie for such a long time, because I've been so stubborn. Because I never wanted to face the truth."

"It's not all your fault, Bel." Ernie crouched down and placed a comforting hand on her arm. "We made a pact. I'm the one who broke it and who wanted you to break it."

"A pact?" repeated Hannah. "What are you talking about?"

"We promised each other," explained Ernie, "never to speak to anyone about what happened that day. Because we could never forgive our- selves for the deaths of those boys. But the guilt was eating me alive. So I went to Martha Cox, not long after it happened, to beg her forgiveness. And she told me that she had never blamed either of us. She tried her best to speak to Bel, to let her know that all she felt towards her was kindness, but Bel always avoided her. She never spoke a word to her again. Or to me. Until today, that is."

"That's why … " whispered Maya. "That's why Martha Cox could never rest in peace. Because Belterre would never forgive herself."

"And I'm so sorry now that I could never bring myself to speak to her while she was alive. You're right, Maya. I've *never* been able to forgive myself. For *anything*."

Hannah scooped up a handful of silky sand and watched it sift through her fingers. "It's a very long time to be carrying around something like that, Bel," she said softly. Ernie Johnson looked over at her, nodded and smiled.

"I know that now," said Belterre, and she buried her face in her hands.

Everyone from the beach gathered back at Willie and Belterre's house that evening, bringing along food from home and pitching in to help Belterre set up a buffet meal. Even Ernie Johnson came back with his wife Betty, as well as a couple of spiny lobsters, to Hannah's father's delight.

It seemed as though Ernie and Bel couldn't get enough of each other. Hannah caught them staring at one another now and then, as if they couldn't believe they were in the same room together, sharing a meal, after so many wasted years. She even saw them hugging once, Ernie's long, gangling arms wrapped soothingly around Bel's comfortable plumpness, his huge hands gently patting her back.

Hannah, Maya and Cassie hadn't found a chance to speak to each other since their return from the beach. Distracted by the bustling kitchen and the buzz of conversation, they even managed to avoid meeting each other's eyes. Whenever Hannah glanced in Maya's direction, Maya would be watching her warily, then her eyes would flick away. And Jake continued to hover around Cassie like a pesky fly until Hannah almost felt like swatting him. When he finally got involved in the chequers tournament starting up at the kitchen table, the three girls all seemed to recognise that the moment had come and they slipped out into the garden.

Hannah and Maya sat on the cedar bench with Cassie cross-legged on the ground in front of them, scarcely visible in the December darkness. No one spoke. The Bermuda breeze sighed through the pawpaw tree, almost as if it were whispering *say something, say something*. But Hannah was waiting. Waiting for someone else to speak first.

"Hannah?"

For an instant she wasn't sure if it was just the wind she was hearing. Then she realised that it was Cassie, whose soft voice had barely penetrated the silence. Then she started to ramble.

"I'm so sorry you had to rescue me today. It's just that I panicked when the water got too high. I thought maybe I could make it back to shore. I've been having swimming lessons, but I forgot everything I ever learned and I was sinking like a stone. Something made me keep on kicking, though, and I managed to hold my nose above the water. But I was so scared." She paused and Hannah heard her sigh. "You're not mad at me, are you? You've been so quiet since it happened."

"She's not mad at you. She's mad at me," said Maya. "Because she found out the truth about you, Cassie, that you've only been living here since the autumn. But we were going to tell you the truth tomorrow, Hannah. Honest." She reached for Hannah's hand and grasped it reassuringly. "Like I already told you, we wanted you to see how crazy it was to be afraid of moving here."

Hannah sat silently in the dark, considering Maya's words. It had just been a silly prank, and a good one, too, when she added it all up. Cassie was proof that it wasn't so tough to adjust to island life. And Hannah had the added benefit of having spent so much time in Bermuda already – all those sun-drenched summers she spent here growing up. She knew the island almost as well as Maya, who was a native! Living here for two years wouldn't be such a huge stretch of time.

"I'm not really mad at either of you," she admitted finally. "Sure, it's been bugging me a bit that you let me believe Cassie has always lived here. But it's myself that I'm mad at, mostly. Ever since we got here, I've been looking for an excuse to be miserable, trying to find all kinds of reasons to turn myself against the island. Believe me, it wasn't easy. For every bad thing, I seemed to find a good thing. So guess what? I've finally decided that, when we move here after Christmas, I'm going to enjoy every single second of the two years we'll be living here!"

"You know what?" said Maya, squeezing Hannah's hand again. "I always knew that deep down you were really an island girl! Welcome home, Banana!"

"Thanks, Papaya," said Hannah. "Now how about those braids you promised me…"

That night, just before turning out the light, Hannah unfolded her Bermuda list. She read each of the columns slowly, considering the words she had written at home in Canada just a few short weeks ago.

I can't believe I spent so much time worrying about this stuff, she thought. *And that I wasted so much time being miserable.* She smiled when she saw the circle of red ink around the words *possibly no friends.* So much had changed since the day she'd drawn that circle. Even the list didn't seem so important any more, with all of its *bad points* that had clouded her true feelings about the island.

Ever since the day she saw Martha Cox on the road, everything had been different. Better, somehow. It was almost as if she became a friend. As if she had wanted Hannah to help her sort out and tidy up fifty years of sadness and misunderstanding between herself and Ernie and Bel. As if she was teaching Hannah to appreciate the beauty of this place.

Hannah scanned the list one more time. Then, slowly, she tore it into tiny pieces and let them flutter through her fingers into the wastebasket beside her bed.

"Welcome home, Hannah," she murmured, as she turned out the light.

And, as she lay there in the dark, Hannah was sure that – just for a moment – the comforting scent of flowers filled the air.